"*A meshumad*–a willing convert—in the family!" Esther spat out the words with all the hatred of the ages . . .

. . . the hatred of those forced to become Christians by threats of death or torture . . . of those who had died . . . and those who lived in constant resistance.

And deep below was the memory of her own years of suffering in a remote Russian ghetto. The Jewishness within her was ever present, a continuous part of her thinking . . . her reactions . . . her life.

How had David wrenched himself from it?

David C. Cook Publishing Co.
ELGIN, ILLINOIS—WESTON, ONTARIO

ESTHER
© David C. Cook Publishing Co.

Published by David C. Cook Publishing Co.,
Elgin, IL 60120
Edited by Janet Hoover Thoma
Cover photo by Wayne Hanna
Designed by Kurt Dietsch
Printed in the United States of America
Library of Congress Catalog Number: 78-57640
ISBN: 0-89191-130-8

CONTENTS

To Tell the Story

Toward the end of her eighty-eight years, Esther Bronstein began to dictate her story into a tape recorder. Someone transcribed it, and someone else rearranged the words and the sentences and put in the proper punctuation. Then a friend sent it to us.

It was a teaser, an appetizer, just enough to tell us that in that life was a powerful and moving story.

Our editors then made several trips to talk to Esther, exploring her past, testing her amazing memory, probing and wandering through closed and half-forgotten pages of history. We had fallen in love with her and were determined to tell her story the best way we knew how, when God called her home.

We then turned to a free-lancer, Maggie Mason, who poured over the transcripts of our interviews, conducted dozens of her own, hunted miles of library shelves for background material, and wrote the first draft. Janet Thoma, a David C. Cook editor, picked up many of the chapters of Esther's life and expanded the story. Both writers approached the task with a sense of privilege in having a part in its telling. They faced a problem, however. The passage of time made it impossible to accurately reproduce conversations, descriptions, and the details of certain incidents, so they used their imagination. David Bronstein, Jr., helped immeasurably with this and in assuring that the final work remained faithful to the character, personality, and accomplishments of both Esther and David Bronstein.

1 THE PALE

"IF GOD LIVED ON EARTH, people would break out all his windows."

So holy was he that they could not speak his name, yet no *shtetl* Jew felt restrained in a hearty argument with the Almighty who had, all things considered, dealt an uneven portion to his chosen people.

And after all the fuss they went to for him—what with the 613 *mitzvat, davening* three times a day, the endless washing, the studies at shul . . .

So they complained, but with an affection and a sense of humor which they were convinced the Holy One, blessed be his Name, shared.

ESTHER

Since the time of the Christian Crusades in the eleventh, twelfth, and thirteenth centuries, the Jews of Central Europe had moved toward the east. At first they were welcomed for the skills they brought. Yet they never mingled, never became part of their Slavic hosts. The incoming Jews even kept their own language, the *mama-loshen*, "mother tongue"—a medieval German often overtaken by Hebrew and carrying hints of the Romance language. They included only as much Slavic as they needed to do business with their neighbors.

Generations came and passed; still they lived apart, scorning the worship of icons and the Gentiles' Jesus, whose followers had shown them nothing but unreasoning hatred and death.

Perhaps as a result of their exclusiveness—and certainly contributing to it—the countries they inhabited placed a series of restraints upon them once their education, their holdings, their business acumen, and their numbers increased. So their lot changed, according to the whim of various rulers.

In 1791 Catherine the Great herded them into the Pale, a three thousand-mile wide plain in southwest Russia where they huddled for protection and identity in their ghetto villages. By the late nineteenth century more than five million Jews lived in some eight hundred villages—villages separated by barren fields and scrub pine alive with wolves and bears. Outside the Jewish portion of the *shtetlach* and tilling the hopeless soil between were miserable peasants whose lot was scarcely better than the Jews.

So they survived. Shut in. Cut off. The *shtetl* served as an incubator, keeping alive the *Yiddishkeit* ("Jewishness") that had been gradually diluted among their kinsmen who remained in the West. There was a kind of eternal obstinacy about them. Except for their faith and their wit, they had little else to sustain them.

Living on the edge of fear, still they joked. Surrounded and infiltrated by those who hated them, they reveled in ingenious Yiddish curses on anyone who was not a Jew, the *goyim*–curses made more effective because they were uncomprehended.

Separated from the culture and education of the progressing world "beyond the Pale," they made their own. Denied the security of life and possessions, they closed in upon themselves in a unity of common misery. . . . And they constantly confided the irony of this situation to a God who was as familiar as their neighbor in the next mud-walled hut and who enjoyed the joke as much as they.

Yet while they survived, they also suffered a stagnation that led to closed minds, jealousies, and rifts over trifling interpretations of the Talmud's sixty-three books. To be a *hasmid* was even better than being rich. To have a daughter marry such a scholar, a man would dower away his possessions. And to be wealthy enough to sit in the synagogue and pray or discuss the Holy Books with the learned men seven hours every day, that would be as Tevye sang in *Fiddler on the Roof,* "the sweetest thing of all."

And that is exactly what many did—not just the rich—while their wives were in the marketplace earning such as they could to support the family. The high value placed on studying the Holy Books contributed to a family balance where, although the father was in authority and the spiritual head of the house, the mother was often more capable of practical decisions, more aggressive, and more assertive.

So intellects that might have opened the door to discoveries in science, technology, philosophy, and human understanding turned inward, leaving these advances to their descendants. The *shtetl* Jews eventually scorned secular knowledge and retreated into a dogged piety, considering themselves God's hostages for the redemption of mankind. The maintenance of their life-style, their religious customs, their language, even their dress, was frozen in forms they found familiar and therefore comfortable.

Then came a ruler who looked more favorably on them—Czar Alexander II, who reigned from 1855 until his assassination in 1881. He permitted a few of their young people to enter universities and opened some travel to the Jews. But they were still the despised *Zyhd,* only tolerated among outsiders. Some retreated even further into the life they knew. Some were absorbed, "passing" as Gentiles. Others, herded again into the Pale, brought with them a ferment of hope, curiosity, and discontent that disturbed the resignation of the most remote *shtetl.*

Thus the growing socialism that rocked the center of Russia reached into the Pale and captured the imagination of their young, giving Alexander III a reason to initiate a series of vicious pogroms. Massacres and organized looting of Jewish synagogues and cemeteries were designed to drain off the revolutionary energy of the peasants, diverting it from their government to the ever-available, captive scapegoats. The result? During the forty years after 1880 more than one-third of the Jewish population migrated—90 percent of them to the United States.

Into such a time and place Esther Peltz and David Bronstein were born. Their lives were not unlike those around them. Only the way God eventually spoke to them was different, and what he called them to do. A task unimaginable to those who had gone before them. And a call heard by only a few.

David was born in 1886 in Rishkanovky, a typical *shtetl* in the heart of Bessarabia, Russia. The middle son of three boys, he was raised in an orthodox Jewish home and enrolled in a Hebrew *cheder* when he was only five. His family migrated to the States about the turn of the century as their sons reached military age. But little else is known about David's early life. His story was less articulated, and as you come to know him you'll understand why.

Esther Peltz was born in 1889 in the *shtetl* of Nikolayev—which she persisted in calling Mikolayev, a tacit denial of any connection with the hated Czar Nicholas II. The village of about fifteen hundred can still be found seventy miles north of the present port of Odessa on the Black Sea. The wretched *shtetl* was torrid in summer, bitter in winter. In the long, arid summers its streets were hazy with yellow dust, which in the spring thaws turned to sucking, miring mud called *shtetlblot*.

The town was livened, however, by an active market where Russian peasants brought their fruits and vegetables to trade for the imports and manufactured necessities their Jewish neighbors acquired. Meat was brought in live for the local *shochet* to examine and slaughter according to the strictest kosher codes.

So there existed a balance of mutual need between the local peasants and these Jews, developing sometimes into a grudging respect. The Russian might even earn the name of *fayner goy*, "an OK fellow." Or, if he could nearly outwit his Jewish counterpart, the term *kluger goy*, "smart fellow," served as both a compliment and a challenge.

The Peltz family were honored participants in this village life. Their home was better than most of their neighbors: made of brick and set on a hill somewhat apart from the rest of the *shtetl* houses.

Esther was the third of eleven children born to Israel and Hindl Peltz (of which only eight lived). Their father, a skilled furrier, bought furs from peasant trappers and made fur hats and coats, which were valued by the Russians and found a ready market in nearby cities. He employed about thirty of the *shtetl* men and taught his sons the trade as they outgrew the village school.

By 1901 the possibility of war with Japan added to the fear that overwhelmed *shtetl* Jews like Israel Peltz. The czar was building his war machine, and Israel and his sons feared that young Jews would be favored as foot soldiers since they were allowed to do little else.

So mothers and fathers fretted after their manner while their youth became more restive and unpredictable because of their socialistic ideas and the impending war. The Peltz family was part of this seething edge.

Z CONSCRIPTION

A HAZE OF YELLOW DUST hung in the darkening streets of Nikolayev. Men and older boys in much-pressed *Shabbes* clothes—their black broad-rimmed hats bobbing in rhythm to their trudging walk—merged for their pilgrimage to the *shul*, the synagogue. Every window gleamed with the holy glow of Sabbath candles. And as each door opened the warm odor of burning wax—pungent and spicy—and the sweet, yeasty smell of cooling bread mingled with the glow and the dust.

A spring breeze fanned the firm young faces of Morris and Harry, the older Peltz brothers, and even penetrated the abundant beard of their father, as they stepped from the house at the head of the street. Esther hesitated as she closed the door, watching her father and brothers. Surely the finest in the whole *shtetl,* they were!

The two young men tall and dark, their high cheek-bones and straight, almost patrician, noses adding to their dignity. And her father. He reminded her of Abraham and the other wise patriarchs. His fully-bearded face held deep-set searching eyes, and his squarish build reinforced the feeling of competence and continuity that surrounded him. A real lion of Judah, he.

At last she turned to the long table where candles burned, dripping wax on the white cloth. The scant remains of their supper were yet to be cleared away—with the least possible work. For *Shabbes* had arrived, and with it blessed relief from labor.

The younger children—Saul, Jacob, Ida, and Ruth—played quietly. Their mother had removed the soft kerchief, which once a week distinguished her priestess function in lighting the candles, and was slumped in a chair beside the table. Esther felt for mama: she worked too hard!

Every Friday it was so—getting the men's Sabbath clothes ready, baking the week's bread, and cleaning the house while she cared for the children. Esther did what she could, but the burden and worry always fell on mama.

But something about Hindl Peltz's drooping shoulders seemed to convey more than work-weariness. An ache of the soul, maybe, that contrasted vividly with Esther's buoyancy.

"Rest, mama," Esther said, her voice more commanding than an eleven year old's should be. Her firm, strong-boned hands quickly cleared the table.

Ah, she thought, *if only things were as peaceful as they seem.* Sometimes her parents talked about the days when they were young—before the kindly czar had been assassinated. Life had been different then—but it would probably never be like that again.

The pogroms had begun again. Esther could remember little else: the drunken thugs who beat or murdered indiscriminately. The menacing sight of mounted ranks of Cossack soldiers killing and destroying with a precision that was even more fearful because it had been planned. Where was the Almighty the men hurried to pray to?

Hadn't her father risen early that morning—and every morning she could remember—put his prayer shawl over his shoulders and murmured: "Hear O Israel, the Lord, our God, the Lord is One," just as Jews had for over twenty-five hundred years?

Esther didn't understand why God seemed to ignore them. Nor might she ever, even though her heart reached out to God as she questioned him.

But not all the changes in the last years had been bad. Somehow a breath of air was stirring the monotony of their village. New thoughts of freedom and the worth of the common people seemed to be seeping through all of Russia, even into the sheltered Jewish villages. Yet she dreaded the emotions these stirrings aroused in their close-knit family. Her older brothers became unpredictable and argumentative when they talked of human dignity and freedom. Her father, like many of the older Jews, seemed threatened by their unrest and discontent. To the older Jews, their misery seemed almost preferable to change. At least it was familiar, and permitted them to continue their unbroken worship of the God who had set them apart.

Just recently there had been talk about a strange quarrel between Russia and Japan. Esther knew little about this.

ESTHER

The Yiddish newspapers only hinted at trouble that might come—possibly even war. But the czar's soldiers made it plain enough when they rode through the *shtetls* looking for Jews of military age.

Jewish men were not considered fit for respected professions, but they would provide diversion for enemy cannon fire. Time and again conscriptors raided their village, carrying away the best of their young men. Surely Morris could not escape for long.

"I will not fight for the czar!" she had heard him say often, with angry determination. "I will not go!"

Esther didn't know which was worse: the thought of his going or the threat implied in his anger. She glanced toward her mother to share her feelings, but mama was now asleep, her head on her folded arms.

After Morris there would be Harry. She shuddered, knowing that her brothers' danger was part of the gloom that burdened her mother. Yet mama was so patient. She never differed with their papa, while Esther spoke her mind, arousing the teasing, loving contempt of her older brothers.

Everybody knew that girls didn't count. Of course they were to be valued and loved. But the attitude of their pint-sized sister never failed to amuse the Peltz brothers. And when she shook her head in frustrated anger they called her "little *nudnik.*" But as often as not they "chose" to follow her ideas.

Sometimes Esther wished that she could be suitably yielding like her mother. Or maybe she wished that her mother could be more like Sadie Krentz down the street, who maneuvered her menfolk without their being aware of it. Or so she thought. But her mother was so gentle. Sometimes, Esther felt more the mother to her.

"*Shah! Shah!*" she cautioned the children, her finger to her lips. "Let mother sleep!" She covered the *kugel,* this

18

time a pudding of noodles left from the evening meal, and carefully placed it on a shelf in the fireplace where it would keep warm. From now until sundown after *Shabbes* there would be no cooking nor even a stirring of the carefully banked fire.

Esther felt different from the other girls in the *shtetl.* She had the same dark hair and full-bodied build. And her high cheekbones resembled the other girls, although her face was rounder and her features softer. Physically, she was not unique. The difference was hidden inside her, in her desire to learn.

She was one of the few girls who went to the village school until she could read Russian and do her figures. And one of still fewer who sat among the boys in the *cheder* learning Yiddish and a little Hebrew.

As she leaned against the warmed-through brick walls of their huge fireplace, she wondered about life outside the *shtetl.* Some day . . . Yet she could go no further. Life outside was beyond her imagination. Still she could not see her "some day" being like today or yesterday—living and dying in this same repetitive pattern. Thousands had done that before her. And thousands might after her—if thousands lived.

But in a way, she knew she should be satisfied here. Her family was respected. Her father's advice was valued, and she herself was often the center of a group of women in the balcony of the *shul,* reading to those who could not read for themselves. Her mother's weariness was pushing Esther into more and more responsibility, which she welcomed—even though she was only eleven. She seemed to grow stronger as the burdens multiplied.

It didn't happen as they thought it might. Just one day . . . Morris was gone.

Papa came home early that evening from Proskurov, the market town where he and Morris had gone to sell their furs.

"Is Morris home?" he called as he entered the door.

Mama turned from kneading the bread. "No. He went with you. . . ." Her voice trailed off in apprehension.

"He said he didn't feel well, so I told him to go back to the hotel and rest. Then when I went to pick him up, he wasn't there."

Her mother's face turned as white as the flour. "He's done it! He's gone!" And she fell into the arms of her husband, wailing her grief and gripping his shoulders with her flour-covered hands.

"Oh! So dreadful! He's so young! My boy, my child!"

"He isn't a child, Hindl. And if he's gone, he only did what he had to do. But we don't know anything yet," papa replied, trying to calm her.

Suddenly she straightened, her face hard with anger. "It's that Sprintzie—that's who! She persuaded him to run away. I never liked that girl. She'll do him no good."

Papa didn't deny her suspicions, though he had always been more tolerant of the girl. Like any good Jewish mama, Hindl wanted her sons to marry into a comfortably prosperous family, which Sprintzie's was not.

"I've wondered about that," papa agreed. "I'm going now to talk to her father."

It seemed hours before he returned. Esther held back her own tears, watching her mother's endless pacing as she calmed the younger children. All the while she pretended, *It isn't happening! It isn't happening!*

One look at her father's face when he opened the door, and she knew it was true. The full story came out slowly, interrupted frequently by her mother's cries of anger and sorrow.

Sprintzie's father had borrowed money for her dowry,

and she and Morris were this minute in the station at Proskurov, waiting for the train to take them out of Russia. They were headed for America. Morris had some money saved and had taken it with him the day before.

But mama would not let them leave without one last attempt to stop them. She rehearsed her strategy through the night instead of sleeping. Then when it was scarcely daylight, she had the hired buggy brought around so she and papa could begin the long trip to Proskurov. Not for two days did Esther learn of the scene in the depot, where they found the two young people sleeping among their bundles as they waited for the train to Riga.

In spite of his mother's tears and arguments, Morris would not be dissuaded. Nor was Esther sure he should have been. She disliked Sprintzie, too, though for reasons other than her mother's. But she was still glad her brother had escaped the czar's men.

So Morris and his girl were on their way to America, pledging, "We'll get rich and send back money for you to come. You'll see!"

But there was an irreparable hole in the family. Mama would talk of nothing else, her eyes were red with crying; and when a year later Harry followed Morris, the family suffered a strange mixture of loneliness, relief that their sons were not in the czar's army . . .

. . . and pride.

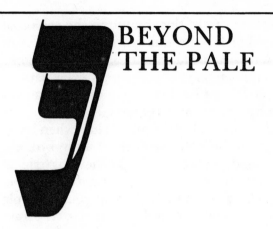

BEYOND THE PALE

EVEN MAMA COULD NOT RESTRAIN a note of superiority when she spoke of "my sons in America." And when the letter carrier arrived with envelopes stamped with an American postmark, everyone in the *shtetl* knew.

Often a crowd would gather around Esther and her mother when Sabbath services were over. Everyone listened as Esther read the latest news, first from New York and later from a place called Baltimore, where already many of their *landsleit,* their fellow countrymen, were living. Esther glowed with pleasure as her mother showed photographs of her handsome sons.

"A *mench,* to be sure!" Molly Feller commented, impressed by their dignity.

A more critical Sarah Goldstein muttered. "But look, no *payees!* Jews, are they?"

Instead of the long, unshorn hair and sideburns worn by Orthodox Jews, the young immigrants had flourishing mustaches and wore short jackets with gold-draped watch chains and derby hats.

Of course, Esther defended them. But in her heart, she was confused. America had changed them so much and so quickly! And the envelopes seldom contained the money they had promised to send.

As proud as her mother seemed when others were around, in the quiet of their home Hindl grieved for her sons. More and more she felt the pull to America. Not the pogroms, not the dismal *shtetl* life could shake her loose. But her sons did. She would have left any day to reunite her family.

For Israel, the decision was not so simple. He was prosperous in Nikolayev and able to provide well for his family. Although his dark hair disguised it, he was nearly sixty-five years old. Could he begin again? Could he feed his family and put down roots in America?

Oy! The stories that came to them! America was in everybody's mind. Even his children played at emigration. Esther brought booklets home from the marketplace—booklets circulated by the steamship companies describing the comforts of the voyage, the opportunities in the new land.

Even the rabbi told of that faraway place where a passage from their Torah was inscribed on a great bell: "Proclaim liberty throughout the land to all the inhabitants thereof." Was this not, he said, what they and their fathers had been seeking?

Israel began to think that maybe this place was the Lord's doing—a place where they were free to be Jews without fear of persecution.

Yet, remembering the restive young men in his congregation, the rabbi went on to warn: "If you go to this land of freedom, do not let freedom mislead you. Remain loyal Jews always."

That was all well and good for the young. But what was an old man to do? Given his choice, Israel would have remained. But Hindl's grief wore at his heart, and Esther and the younger ones pressed their own propaganda on him.

One day he called on the rabbi in private.

"Nearly four years have passed since Morris left," he said. "I have six children yet at home. You know we now have an infant son. Since Joey's birth, which I hoped would console Hindl, she only seems to grieve more. What shall I do?"

The *rabbi* was no stranger to this problem.

"Have you thought of going alone?" he asked. "You could get settled, find a job and a home, and then send for your family. Your shop boss would keep your business running. And Esther is a young woman now." He smiled. "Quite a shop boss herself, and capable of caring for her mother."

Israel didn't dare give Hindl any hope until he had made up his mind. He found Esther alone one night after her mother had gone to bed. She was only fifteen, yet seemed a woman as she busied about, getting the children's clothes ready for the next day. For a while he watched her strong arms, her quick, certain step, and her brown curls that never seemed to stay put. Then he began to express his doubts.

"What shall I do, my child? Shall I go to America? Can I provide for my family there? Will we lose our Jewishness?"

"You'll never know until you try, *tata*. Saul and I can manage here. And I really fear for mama unless she has hope of getting our family together."

So Israel Peltz packed his boxes for the bone-shaking cart ride to Proskurov, the eight-hundred-mile train trip to Riga, and the long ocean journey to the land that not only had a freedom bell but a great lady with a torch, who stood in the harbor and welcomed the immigrant.

Esther was the head of the home now—older than her remaining brothers and stronger than her ailing mother. At fifteen, she accepted full responsibility for the family. But she did not mind. Not at all! The role suited her. Their life in the *shtetl* had already been molded into a pattern. All she had to do was follow it, with the security of the body of God's people around her. Only at nights when mama was unusually depressed or at times when the Russian harassment erupted into violence did the burden seem too much.

When the message to come arrived in early 1905, she already had her plans made.

It wasn't hard to sell the house and business. She got a good price and hoarded her store while she negotiated with an agent for passage to America for the seven of them: mama, herself, Saul, Jacob, Ida, Ruth, and two-year-old Joey. The travel service even included help with the packing and checking their belongings through to their Baltimore destination—first by cart, then train, and finally on the boat.

But what should they take? Esther pondered, weighing the value of each piece against the cost and burden of shipping or carrying—now and then yielding to her mother's "I must keep that!" Eventually they sold all their furniture, keeping only their clothing, their brass and copper ware, some fine dishes, and their precious goosefeather pillows and feather beds.

ESTHER

As they sold and packed, Esther noted with growing alarm the ashen tone of her mother's face and the sudden, fierce twistings of pain that gripped her now and again.

Mama still looked healthy. Her hair was darker than papa's, and her face still held the proud, aristocratic bearing that Esther and her two brothers had inherited. But the fatigue that Esther used to notice at the end of a long day now came in the early afternoon and much more frequently.

"Mama, are you sure you can stand the journey?" Esther couldn't help but ask.

"Silly child! Of course! And you'll see. I'll be as good as new when I'm with your father again."

But Esther was only half convinced by her mother's protestations. And she was worried that her mother didn't realize how much her brothers might have changed in the years they had been gone—nearly five now, for Morris. Even in the *shtetl* a young man changed in five years. And in America? If their pictures or the tone of their letters were any indication . . . There was little mention of *shul* or studies, only good times and work and new friends.

But in lighter moments she, too, believed that her mother would be better in America—if only she could bear the journey. So Esther made it as easy as possible for her, taking the burden of the decisions and acquiring the passport.

The day when the heavy, two-wheeled carts rolled up to the door came all too soon. The draymen carried out their crates and bundles. Each child had his burden to carry. And then there were clothes for the journey.

"The food we'll buy in Hamburg," she told Jacob, whose first concern always seemed to be what he would eat next. "I've been told the food on the ship is not only *trayf* (not kosher), but could also make us sick."

Neighbors waved from their doorways, and tears mingled with joy as the wagon lumbered down the familiar streets. Their agent rode with the carts, which weary horses pulled at a plodding gait.

"Are you sure your mother is all right?" he asked Esther. And Esther reassured him, worrying all the while whether he could cancel his agreement at the last minute. But by the time they arrived at Proskurov, she knew the journey would push her mother to the end of her endurance. So she bullied and cajoled Saul and Jacob into taking more responsibility for the younger children.

Esther had only seen a train once before, and when they reached the station, she had no notion of how to proceed. Nor had she faced so many strange faces before. No matter how she assumed control of the family, she could not overcome her fear of strangers. In the village, strangers usually meant harassment—or worse. She instinctively distrusted anyone she had not known for years; now she was surrounded by them.

But as soon as their agent had supervised the unloading of their carts, he maneuvered them aboard the train and vowed to see them through to Hamburg. His service, Esther decided, was well worth the cost. As long as he did not desert them, she felt fairly safe.

The train for Riga was noisy and dirty, but at least the children could move in the aisles or sleep, sprawled over their precious bundles. At every stop Esther counted the bundles, fearful always lest one be stolen or forgotten.

For the first miles, the ancient engine labored in a steady climb. Then the land leveled off—high, rolling, monotonous—stretching endlessly to the brown horizon. There was little to see until they reached the rich grasslands of the upper Ukraine where fat cattle grazed. Here the homes were made of wood. And the air felt clean and fresh in their lungs when they stopped for a break.

When the train stopped to take on fuel and water at one breezy upland station, Esther escaped to run along the platform. Then, with a cautious look at the train, she jumped down to feel the cool grass under her feet.

"Isn't this fun!" she called to her brothers, but they were far behind and half in a stupor from lack of sleep and the humming of the wheels.

At last the great port of Riga rose against the deep blue of the Baltic. There would be a ship waiting to take them to Hamburg.

But a shipping strike held them there for sixteen days while Esther watched her precious gold pieces disappear in hotel bills and meals. Nor was the ordeal ended when they sailed around the point into Hamburg, the German port of embarkation for America. For there they must pass the rigid inspection of emigration officials before receiving their visas for America.

Again they huddled together in a blur of strange faces. Only this time, many of the faces had the familiar characteristics of their people. That helped to ease Esther's terror as the travel agent bid them good-bye. A *goy* he might be. But honest he also was, and she thanked God for that.

Now they faced the endless inspection lines—in terror and apprehension. The small children showed their nervousness by quibbling and fighting among themselves, Esther by snapping back at them over the slightest irregularity. She had taken special care to make sure everyone was clean. Now they wanted to sit or play on the floor. The more exhausted they became, the more she sympathized with them. Finally, she gave in. But by the time they reached the doctors, she prayed they would pass—especially mama.

Ida and Ruth went first. No problem there. Esther

motioned for mama to go ahead. If she failed, Esther wanted to be close by to reason with the doctors, to cajole, or do whatever she could to influence them. But even mother, who seemed to muster a special strength for the ordeal, passed. Feeling the joy that accompanies relief, Esther watched her move toward the outer waiting room. There was no way Esther would fail. She knew it.

But as she left the women's inspection room, still buoyed by their success, Jacob rushed toward her, his face strained with emotion. Saul—fourteen-year-old Saul—had been rejected! The doctors said it was an eye condition. Trachoma. He would not be allowed to go to America until it cleared.

Esther hurried through the crowd to her mother. But even from a distance she saw that mama already knew.

"Gott in Himmel! What shall we do?" mama was wailing when Esther reached her. "My boy, my Saul!"

This fresh blow seemed to open all the old grief. And the courage she had gathered for her own examination melted.

Esther took her in her arms. "Now, mama, we'll do what we can" . . . when all the while she knew there was no way she could keep Saul with them, nor would their funds allow them to wait in Hamburg for the weeks or months that might be necessary for his treatment.

As she soothed her mother, she searched for an answer. Surely there was someone who could help, someway they could proceed and still leave Saul in good hands. There must be *landsleit* in Hamburg—others traveling to some port that would allow Saul to enter. Where were the faces that had looked so familiar?

Sure enough, Jewish loyalty came through. As she inquired, one person directed her to another, until she eventually found the Kaplans from Odessa. They were on their way to Liverpool. Papa had often done business with them. And Saul had even visited their home. They had a son about his age.

Soon Mrs. Kaplan added her comfort to Esther's. "Ease yourself, Mrs. Peltz. We will take care of Saul as our own son."

Esther watched in tired resignation as with new tears and more worries Hindl Peltz kissed another son good-bye. Would she ever see him again? Esther didn't want to contemplate the possibility.

Besides the love they held for Saul, Esther knew his absence would be doubly hard on her. He was the next oldest, the one she leaned on most. If the family had a male in any authority, it was Saul. Now he, too, was gone. Esther felt like her forebears in the wilderness: God seemed to be testing her, almost to the breaking point. But where was the manna to sustain her?

Soon they were on the S.S. *Hamburg,* with a generous supply of sardines to supplement such shipboard food as their kosher diet would allow them to eat. They were assigned a room above deck—with two children who were traveling alone and could not proceed without an adult sponsor. The room was crowded, the air close and stale, but it was infinitely better than steerage.

"You go get our ration, Jacob," Esther said the second day out, when the choppy English channel downed everyone with seasickness. Though queasy, she did not suffer severely, nor did Jacob. But she did not dare leave the others.

So each day Jacob trudged off, with little Joey behind him, to get their day's kosher rations, which usually consisted of black bread, herring, and potatoes.

There was a reason for taking two-year-old Joey, for he got a ration of milk. In fact, other women borrowed him for their turn in line, and the busy cooks ladled his portion out again and again without ever realizing it.

They had to buy water for both bathing and drinking. Others risked the salty sea water for washing, but Morris had written a warning: "It will cause redness of the eyes, and I saw people turned away on Ellis Island because of that. Be sure to bathe only in fresh water!"

Gradually the children recovered from their nausea. In the more gentle movement of the ocean they needed only to be kept clean, fed, entertained, and out of harm's way.

Esther pitied the steerage passengers who were allowed on deck only for a short period each day. The stench from the passageways and the forlorn, hopeless people who emerged convinced her that their third-class passage had been a good investment. Steerage would have cost only thirty-four dollars a person, and she had paid much more. But they would be on board for thirteen long weeks. And she knew now that her mother could not have survived more stress. For though the children became accustomed to the sea, mama never did. Each day they watched her become more and more wan and thin.

Esther cried at night after everyone was asleep. She was becoming convinced that mama's health had been broken. Slowly she began to wish for the support of someone stronger than herself. She had carried this burden for almost a year now. And each month, each day, seemed to be harder. Would it never end? Would she ever be able to relax again? She might not even be as free with her advice to her father and brothers, now that she knew how hard it was to be in control.

Her brothers' teasing was part of a security she tried to imagine each night, to relieve the tension she felt and ease herself into sleep.

But by day she forced her fears deep within so she could continue. And each day the children quarreled.

They were fretful in their confinement. They made pests of themselves with the other passengers, or she was afraid they would. They tired of the food. They shirked their small portion of the daily tasks. But she was strict, very strict. She would separate the combatants with *"Nu, nu, nu . . .!"* at once soothing and threatening.

She made up stories to pass the time. Endless stories. Stories from the Bible, with original, heretical embellishments. Stories of people they had left behind. Magical stories about the new land that would welcome them, where it was said even the floors were covered with velvet nicer than a rich man's table.

Then one day the gulls came out to meet the boat. Esther, Jacob, and a hundred or so other hearty souls were up at dawn the next morning—July 4, 1905. And there she stood, just as the travel folders had pictured: the great lady with the torch!

"Oh, see!" Even Jacob was awed into a hushed whisper. The mist lifted. By now there must have been a thousand crowding the rail, straining for their first glimpse of the promised land. Here and there awe gave way to noisy celebration.

"Mazel tov! Mazel tov!" one cried to the other, voicing hearty congratulations in having made it thus far. Others retreated under their white-tassled *tallis* and swayed in fervent, thankful prayer.

Some—possibly the more realistic among them—regarded the approaching shore with taunt face and narrowed eyes. The hazards of escaping Russia, the risk of examination and detainment in Hamburg, even the miseries of the voyage did not compare with the dreaded indignities and confusion that awaited them on Ellis Island. Anxiety that they had denied in their excited preparation, that had been overwhelmed by the immediate suffering of shipboard, must now be met head on.

Each family gathered themselves closely together. Which of them might be denied visa? What unknown, unimaginable nightmare awaited them in those red buildings?

Esther, of all her family, had been coached on bits of wit and wisdom to carry them through this last ordeal. But now she wanted to enjoy the excitement of the moment. With Jacob, she helped their mother to the rail so she could catch her first glimpse of their new home. The great lady was dimmed now by clouds of smoke, but still resplendent.

When they were even nearer yet, Esther lifted little Joey and pointed toward land. "See? America! *Tata's* there!"

Yes, papa was there, and so were Morris and Harry. And now they had joined them. Surely they were entering the promised land.

4 ELLIS ISLAND

THE NEXT MORNING they almost forgot to eat, what with watching the busy tugboats, listening to the whistle signals, and marveling at the greatness of the city just beyond the island they approached. The bright cloudless sky and shining sun seemed to echo everyone's expectations.

Reluctantly, Esther returned to the practicalities that lay ahead. Recognizing the familiar signs, the younger ones tried to slip away in the crowd so they could continue to enjoy the festivities. But Esther's voice carried over the celebration and the prayers, the horns and the churning water.

"Jacob, Ida, Ruth! Come here at once!" They knew that tone and came hurrying to their room, where Esther got her brood cleaned and fed. Then there were bundles to repack and label. Each one was given to the child who could best carry it.

Even mother caught the excitement of landing. Soon their feet would be planted on American soil, and she would be near her husband and sons. As they sat among their bundles to wait, Esther pored over the innumerable warnings and instructions her brothers had sent. How could she remember them all? Most important, would their mother pass the physical examination?

The nearer they approached the island, the more her fears mounted. She struggled to swallow her dry panic.

She was, after all, only sixteen. The ordeal of the admittance procedure was enough to send many adults toward the deep edge of fear. But she was also responsible for six loved ones—plus the two young strays, whom she must help in finding the people who awaited them. One of her six charges was a baby who was half-ill from improper food and confinement. Three were skittish, uncooperative youngsters. And mama was almost too ill to walk down the gangplank. Could her grit carry them all?

She determined they would make it through.

The shipload of immigrants did not know that America was scarcely more prepared to cope with them than they were with America. These strangers were arriving at the rate of nearly 1,200,000 a year, averaging 3,300 a day. And there was that terrible time when 15,000 landed in twenty-four hours. Even on the leanest of days, facilities, officials, and volunteers were tried beyond limits. Boat after boat lined the pier as hordes of travel-weary, sick, confused, and frightened people converged on Ellis Island.

Many national groups had established immigrant aid societies in New York, and their representatives sought out countrymen as they disembarked. The Hebrew Immigrant Aid Society, for instance, had been organized by another generation of Jews, now fixed in America and able to offer advice, loans, jobs, and sometimes even redemption funds for their kinsmen who were held for lack of entry money.

But these helpful societies were vastly overburdened. In no way could every question be answered, every heart-rending problem solved. It was hurry, hurry, don't slow the line, answer the question, stand here, go there—a monstrous shuffling of human destiny that was so shattering it left a permanent memory on even the youngest child.

No doubt some of the immigration staff became hardened by the suffering they saw every day. But most were not heartless. They were overwhelmed. And the only way they could do their job was to consider each frightened, confused bit of humanity as another commodity to be numbered, sorted, and slid down the proper chute with as much speed as possible.

Even before the ship landed, the dehumanizing experience began. Officials boarded and tagged the arrivals—some of whom cowered while others affected a dignified defiance or accepted the procedure with a good-humored resignation. Esther had decided to cooperate in every detail and in no way to attract attention to her little party.

"Hurry! Hurry!" shouted the officials in a dozen languages as they herded the long-confined travelers from the S.S. *Hamburg* onto the customs wharf.

Then they poured into a massive hall that echoed and magnified the din of a hundred dialects and languages. The milling around threatened to separate their family, but Esther shouted her instructions above the roar: "Hold onto each other! Keep your bundles under your arms, and stay in the same line as long as you can!"

Waist-high rails divided the large room into dozens of corridors. Toward the head of each line, she could see those being examined. Their frightened faces telegraphed fear to those waiting behind them. Some were near hysteria. Some stoic. All shuffled toward the inevitable.

As they approached the row of doctors, Esther again relinquished a brother to the men's examining room. Certainly Jacob, who seemed stronger than most of them, would pass. Still she reminded him again of Morris's many instructions.

Then their turn came. The examinations were rapid, but the doctors knew exactly what to look for. Practiced hands felt for abnormalities. A stethoscope, still warm from the person before her, was pressed to heart and lungs, searching for tuberculosis, "the Jew disease." Now she was doubly glad she had kept her family clean, for she saw others with scalp and skin problems marked with chalk and set aside for further examination.

A push into another slot, and a tongue depressor gagged her. Then she heard Joey howl while Ruth and Ida cried in fear as in one quick movement a doctor caught their upper eyelash and rolled their eyelid over a little stick.

But responding to the questions and instructions issued by her own line of examiners kept Esther too busy to watch either the children or her mother. When she did see her mother, she was proud. For Hindl Peltz, this close to reunion with her family, had more color in her face and more assurance to her carriage than Esther had seen in years. Almost healthy, she looked. At least the doctors passed her, and soon the seven of them were together again. Not one had a chalk mark to call them back.

But this was not all. Again they were in lines, now according to nationality. Mercifully, a Yiddish interpreter waited at the desk, but the hurry, hurry, push, push, allowed not a moment for query or explanation.

Questions, with machine-gun rapidity. "Where was your father born? Your mother? Can you read and write? Where are you from? Who is meeting you? Do you have support? Do you have a job? How much money do you have? When were you born?"

This last one stumped Esther. The inspector, recognizing her leadership in the family group, had directed the questions to her. How could she give their birth dates in American months and years when the day of their births had been reckoned as "so many days before Passover" or "so many days after Rosh Hashanah"—and that on a different calendar? For the Hebrew calendar began in September or early October and lasted for thirteen months.

After some quick advice from the interpreter, Esther rattled off the dates as if she knew them, arbitrarily assigning birthdays to each of them. An in-family joke for years to come would be good-natured quarrels about their ages and birthdays. But she did what she could. And they got through.

They stayed overnight on the island, sitting on the rigid benches when they could, walking about when their cramped positions became unbearable. It was hard to be so near and still so far.

In the morning the children gazed hungrily at the vendors who hawked their wares through the masses of waiting people. After their unbroken diet of herring and potatoes, the foods looked delicious. With everyone watching anxiously, Esther approached the next vendor who passed, pointed to some bright oranges, a little box of cheese, and a loaf of bread, and held out a five-dollar gold piece. He gave her the food and some money in return. Was the change right? Was his price fair? Esther suspected not, and determined to learn that part of American life quickly.

Then there was the ferry to arrange for and train tickets for Baltimore to be purchased. She listened carefully as others found answers to their questions, learned who were the right people to ask, and discovered the particular badge that marked people who spoke Yiddish and were stationed here and there, ready with advice and directions.

Once they left New York, the train ride to Baltimore was very different from their long journey through Russia. They passed through immaculate little towns, where everybody must surely be rich. Hills, lush with ripening crops or grand with towering trees, slipped by on either side of the train. The ride was short, and some of it at night, so the children slept. But Esther's sleep was the most profound. One moment she was watching a village in the last of the twilight sun; the next, the children were shaking her awake, laughing. Already she felt the role of authority slipping from her. "The train man said Baltimore is next," Ida and Ruth yelled excitedly.

Quickly she recovered her dignity. *"Hoo, ha!"* she cried, scolding affectionately. "We can't let *tata* see us like this!" And she sent them off one by one to the tiny washroom. Then she tucked her hair under her scarf, smoothed her sleep-wrinkled dress, and looked up to see her mother smiling at her.

"Thank you, my darling. You have done so well. I'm sorry I couldn't help more."

Esther felt her lower lip tremble. She was terribly tired of being in charge. Soon she would be free.

For many others on the train, Baltimore was the end of

the journey. Every day immigrants arrived—most of them, like the Peltzes, Jews from Eastern Europe. As in New York, it was the established German Jews who felt responsible for these kinsmen, who were like strangers to them in appearance, language, life-style, and sometimes even religion.

Still they doggedly manned and financed societies to care for the poor, the sick, the disoriented. Baltimore contained one of the strongest, most loyal, and wealthiest Jewish communities in the United States, nearly fifty thousand strong. They cared for their own, though the new arrivals seemed alien.

These incidentals were of little concern to Esther and her family. Papa and Morris and Harry would be at the station to meet them. Their world was coming together again.

ל TRADITION

ISRAEL PELTZ was by now well established in the New World. After he and Morris and Harry had found one another, they had quickly identified their Jewish *landsleit* and their habitat in Baltimore's "downtown" Jewish community. The "uptown" Jewish area was the more fashionable German-Jewish center.

But they could be comfortable downtown; elsewhere they were "the Russians." Russians! The very name they had hated for centuries! So they clung together with other Eastern European Jews, forming crowded urban *shtetls.*

One such area was the northeast corner of Baltimore,

at one time a middle-class neighborhood. The streets were bordered with narrow row houses that shared common sides, getting their sunlight through roof-windows. Once the friendly, end-to-end porches along the front had entertained quiet family retreats on summer evenings. Now the houses were overrun with immigrants—two, three, and four families crowded into facilities designed for one.

In the evening, bearded, *shtreimel*-topped Jews trudged to the *shuls,* which appeared with frequency as each group of *landsleit* sought out their own and tenaciously fought to hold on to the traditions that had sustained them. For these traditions gave each Jew a sense of who he was and what God expected of him.

But the Jew's struggle to remain the same was lost from the beginning. Factory hours that started early and ended late left little time for *shul.* No longer could the men of the house retreat under the *tallis* for the long recital of morning and evening prayers, while the women and younger members of the family waited in discreet, respectful silence. It took time to wind the long cords of the *tefellin* about their arms and foreheads, binding the leather-boxed scrolls close to their heads and hearts as the Lord—blessed be his name—had directed.

Always the clock ticked away reproachfully. And the family, scattering to jobs and school, could not wait. The ritual devotions that had been part of their lifeblood had no place in the hurry-up, survival society they now endured. Children were shunted into public schools, and brought home a strange language—and even stranger ideas. Their young men found all-night pool halls, saloons, and dance halls. With unaccustomed money in their pockets—for jobs were plentiful if poorly paid—a restlessness that had begun in the churning political changes of Europe found vent in the streets of Baltimore.

Other immigrant groups—the Irish, the Italians, the Swedes, Germans, and Poles—met much the same problems. They handled them differently, coming from a less distinctive society. But the Jew had survived through the centuries by seeming to adapt. His protection lay in making himself invisible, in fading into the landscape. Yet underneath flowed the strong, unchanging current of an eternal religion and a family structure that only seemed to yield. At the core, at the matrix, it never changed.

Contributing to this stability was an unreasoning loyalty within the family, among *landsleit,* and extending out to the thousands of other *shtetl* Jews, whom they did not know but who shared similar traditions—the Holy Books of the Talmud, the Torah scrolls, which arrived in carefully wrapped bundles and had been carried as lovingly as any child through the long voyage, and their unchanging faith.

This faith also bridged the gap between the impoverished, confused newcomers and the settled German Jews who were now second- and third-generation Americans. They particularly loathed the immigrants' Yiddish tongue, which they thought of as a vulgar corruption of their own language. In Baltimore, some of these Jews stood at the top of the social-economic-academic ladder. And though the flood of East Europeans bewildered and embarrassed them, blood and religion bound them to help their own.

Newcomers like the Peltzes and the Bronsteins, who arrived at about the turn of the century, found allies in the Friedenwalds and the Levys, the Hutzlers and the Sonneborns. These families and others maintained homes in Eutaw Place, a beautiful boulevard patterned after the Champs Elysees in Paris. They owned stores, factories, and banks. And they employed thousands. They maintained hospitals, orphanages, and schools.

So the immigrant's first need, a job, was quickly met—maybe even as he stepped down from the train, for "greeners" were hired on the spot. Americans had only recently been caught up in the ready-made clothing fad, and factories in the East could not turn out garments fast enough. A far cry they were from the carefully hand-stitched, hand-fitted garments that were the specialty of European-trained tailors.

Sonneborns in particular had cashed in on this market. By 1902 they employed two thousand five hundred people in an eight-story factory. Huge machines cut the same size and fabrics by the hundreds. Even the most unskilled could run up the seams, pin the pleats, and press the trousers. There were "inside shops"—factories. And "outside shops"—run by a proprietor with small capital who bought bundles of work and maintained a few stitchers and machines in his home or loft. "Sweat work," it was called, and whole families toiled early and late, paid by the piece for each garment they stitched together. Anybody could qualify as a "Columbus tailor."

Under such conditions the slow-paced, intimate family life of the *shtetl* Jew found new forms. Even in the sweat shop a camaraderie of shared misery drew them together. And though the hours were long, they could stop for *Shabbes* and the Holy Days.

The more realistic saw that this state could at best be temporary: it was only delaying the inevitable. For the desire—the need—to Americanize was strong among the Jews. Their hard-learned survival tactic, invisibility, demanded that they assimilate as soon as possible. Yet their identity, changeless as the ages, must be maintained. So the family and the individual struggled between a desire to learn English and love of the *mama-loshen;* between the need to make a living and love of the *shul;* between ambition expressed by education and the more current demand for food and rent money.

At the heart of this identity crisis was the Jewish mother. Trained in the *shtetl* to be practical, to handle the financial affairs of the family, to push the purpose of her family, her role became even more important in América. There was never any doubt as to who was the final arbiter: father was head of the house. But mama took charge. She handled the family's ambivalence. To Americanize meant first of all to educate her children, and she saw in the American schools possibilities far beyond the basic reading, writing, and arithmetic available in the *shtetl.* Here Jews could go to high school and beyond. Already some taught at the great Johns Hopkins University in Baltimore. Education! this was the key to survival and progress.

So she clutched at pennies. She worked long hours after her children were in bed. And she often worked while her husband was at *shul,* for many orthodox men, more deeply entrenched in the religious life, found it much harder to change their Old World pattern than the women did. Some of the older men turned to the *shul* as an unrealistic retreat from the demands of a new life they could not cope with.

But mama coped. She coaxed and threatened her children into regular school attendance and good grades. She patched and scrubbed to maintain respectability and pride. And she edged the family up from one level of ghetto life to another a little better—on another street, perhaps.

As Esther and her charges approached the New World, Ida Bronstein was already coping with this challenge.

She and Jacob, with their three sons, Morris, David,

and Benjamin, lived on Lombard Street when the Peltz men arrived in Baltimore. Like the Peltzes, the Bronsteins were skilled furriers. The boys, much the same age, became friends. Harry and David even found their first work together as pressers at Sonneborn's.

And the Bronsteins opened their home to the Peltz men, increasing Ida Bronstein's duties. Now she cared for seven men—five of them pulling hard into their Americanization and at least one, Israel Peltz, holding fast to the old life.

But about one matter Israel Peltz asserted himself. Teasing—yet in dead earnest as one accustomed to planning his children's future—he constantly bragged, "David, just you wait until you see my Esther!"

And you wouldn't have recognized the Peltz brothers' former *nudnik* in the girl they described to David, who was scholarly and serious and consequently fun to tease about the possibilities of a girlfriend or wife.

Meanwhile Morris Peltz had married his Sprintzie, moved away from the Bronsteins' flat, and soon had a small fur business of his own. He hired his father to match pelts—at no more than he had to pay. Morris was not the most popular among them, but his success was the most rapid, which in itself marked him for respect.

The more studious David Bronstein dealt differently with the swift changes in his life. Even after the other boys had given up their religious habits, he continued his morning and evening prayers—*davening*—which sometimes became a hasty putting on and taking off of the *tefellin*. Tradition held him strongly. But in this strange new environment, tradition—necessary to his faith—was being shaken.

Still, he held on—outwardly religious, inwardly troubled. At the same time, he struggled to Americanize. This struggle was expressed most strongly in his desire to learn English. When he and his new friend Morris Peltz discovered that the English teacher who had been recommended to them held her classes in a Baptist church, he didn't know whether to proceed or turn back. He had already been exposed to Christianity—an exposure not likely to attract him.

There was the time he had been treated to a trip to the city with his father, who would sell his fur pieces there. Exploring, as boys will do, he had seen a procession approaching. White-robed boys carried large brass crosses, which he knew to be religious symbols. Cowled priests followed, swinging censers that wafted the pungent odor of incense. Then came a casket, borne on the shoulders of husky men. And behind them, solemn and tearful mourners.

A religious procession, David had thought, and practicing the respect long a part of his tradition, he had placed the hat he carried on his head and stood aside.

But when the mourners passed, one stepped out of the procession and headed directly for him, his eyes angry. David retreated, apprehensive, and puzzled. But the man reached him and slapped his face, crying, "You Jew! You Christ killer! Show some respect! Take that hat off!"

Those watching opened a path before David, as though he were dirty, when he retrieved his hat from the dust in the street. *Ah,* he thought, *a lesson well learned. These are the Christians father has told me about.*

His next encounter, a few years later, had taught him even more. A Christian missionary had ventured into their community, distributing free books among the Jews. Always a scholar, David had eagerly accepted the gift. But after some reading, he came across elements that disturbed and confused him, so he sought the advice of his aged uncle, a recognized Hebrew scholar.

The older man needed only to glance at the book to see

that it was a Hebrew New Testament. He helped David tear the book apart and burn it, page by page.

His only other contact with Christianity had been through the Russian Orthodox Church. Crosses and icons terrorized any *shtetl* boy, for the cry of "Beat the *Zhid!*" came from the same throats that intoned Christian chants on another day.

But David wanted so much to learn English, and the church was not at all as he had imagined. There were no icons, no crucifix, no images. But his first class in English began with the singing of "When the Roll Is Called Up Yonder."

Gradually, the enthusiasm of others in the class waned until David alone was left. He continued his lessons until someone new came into his life: Esther Peltz. Soon he was too busy to continue.

THE PROMISED LAND

THE TRAIN LURCHED and screeched across the switches, belched insolently into the languid air over Baltimore's railyard, and slipped by standing cars only an arm's length away. Esther felt every turn of the wheels that brought their family closer to reunion. For a while she completely forgot to be in charge. She was a child again, her face pressed against the sooty window, her eyes taking in everything she could see of the city that would be their new home.

After what seemed like hours, the engine wheezed to a stop. They had arrived! Now she had to be a general again, assigning bundles and keeping her six together amidst others who were as eager to leave the train as they.

Jacob was the first down the steps. "There's *tata!*" he shouted, then dropped his burden and ran toward the bearded figure that seemed much older than Esther remembered.

As papa approached, Harry and Morris bounded ahead, and her little party exploded with excitement. But Ida and Ruth did manage to hold onto their bundles as they ran to meet their brothers.

Esther, hesitating between carrying Joey and retrieving what Jacob had dropped, saw mama flush with joy. Then there were strong arms around them and tears and laughter and questions and teasing. And without her having a worry or giving an order, they were quickly stowed away in a cab. Such handsome men, her brothers! What though they didn't look like *shtetl* Jews—they were Americans now. She laughed aloud as she lifted a howling Joey from the arms of a big brother he couldn't remember.

"Mama, this is God's country!" father was saying again. "There's no shame to being a Jew here. No fear!"

How beautiful mama is! Esther thought. And how happy, even when papa explained that their apartment wasn't ready yet and that they would stay with friends for a few days.

The ride was not long. When they turned into streets with houses instead of factories and shops, Esther wondered how the driver would ever know where to stop. All the doorways looked the same—and yes, just as papa had said, everywhere were people like themselves. Surely Baltimore was a wholly Jewish city! Somehow, the driver found the right house and pulled the reins with a sharp "Whoa!"

A kindly woman appeared on the porch as the noisy crowd alighted.

"Welcome!" she said, and Ida Bronstein drew Hindl Peltz into her arms.

Esther saw their hostess stop to wipe her eyes with the corner of her apron before hugging each of the girls. Even Joey responded to Ida Bronstein's greeting, and soon the family, with all their bundles, stepped into the cool of the house, each deferring to the other—with Esther herself quite out of charge. She sat timidly as Mrs. Bronstein served a sweet, cold drink, then followed her hostess upstairs to the plain, clean sleeping rooms she had set apart for them. What a strange window in the roof! But without it the hall would have been quite dark, for the house was shut in from both sides. Esther felt a wave of homesickness for the wide sky of Nikolayev.

Then mama was suddenly tired, like a rubber balloon with a bad leak. Esther left her lying listlessly across the bed, *tata* awkwardly smoothing her hair. He cast anxious, questioning looks at Esther. But she pretended not to notice.

It was much later—after mama had rested and come back downstairs—when the Bronstein men returned. There had been so much to talk about! Not so much, however, but that Harry had drawn Esther aside with, "Just you wait until you see my friend, David!" And so subdued was she, so overwhelmed by all that was new, that she couldn't even manage a proper retort.

Then they were there. Ida Bronstein proudly introduced them. "My husband, Jacob. My sons, Morris, Benjamin . . . Where are you, David?"

All the way home David had been apprehensive. This Esther . . . he would be meeting her. His shyness slowed his steps, keeping him a pace behind the others, and at the last minute compelling him to take cover behind his taller brothers until his mother called him out.

David's and Esther's eyes met across the room, and the

dozen or so people around seemed unimportant. Esther saw the brown, curling hair, the full beard, the sensitive eyes—she knew that look, like the village rabbi and others who loved the Holy Books. His features were fine, his hands not suited to the hard work that consumed his days. She looked full into his eyes. In that moment, she loved him.

And David? The girl he saw exceeded anything her father had described. Lovely. Blooming with health and youth. Or was she blushing? He smiled—he couldn't help it—and a song began in his heart.

If the others noticed, if they exchanged knowing glances, it didn't matter. Esther and David had found the mate God had chosen.

The next morning Esther stayed in her room until she heard the men leave for work. She had listened to every voice, every step on the stair, but she did not dare appear until David had gone. Then there was work—lots of it. Travel-soiled clothes to be washed. A fretful Joey to tend. Curious children to be warned again and again about straying from the porch, for how would they ever find the right house again? New sights, new sounds, and the pleasure of hearing her mother and Mrs. Bronstein chat like old friends.

That Sabbath, the synagogue service was such that they might have been back in Nikolayev. Only a vacant store, it was, and not nearly so beautiful. But it filled a longing for the family.

The next day they were introduced to their apartment, which was on Baltimore Street, just a few blocks away. *Apartment* meant little to Esther, who was accustomed to the large home she had known in Russia. But she soon learned that home was now only three rooms that were reached by two flights of stairs.

The rooms were hot. Close. Dim. And they smelled of

other people's cooking. She saw her father look anxiously toward her mother. He had done his best. To sleep his large family, he had placed a large bed in the living room—that was for mama and papa; two beds in the bedroom, with not even a path between, for the three girls and Joey; and two cots in the kitchen for Jacob and Harry. Then there was a stove and a table, which would never seat the lot of them at once.

They managed. But the crowded life wore on her mother. Esther soon went to work for her brother Morris so they could afford a larger apartment. Jacob and the girls were in school, leaving only Joey at home with mama. Now they were happy just being together. For only Saul was missing, and he had written from Liverpool that he was doing well.

But Esther's fears about mama could no longer be ignored, for she was often sick. She visited a doctor, and they heard the word *cancer*. With their scant knowledge of English, it didn't carry its full weight. Meanwhile, Esther watched mama lag more each day. That, and her differences with Morris about her wages, were her only problems. She was sure Morris was cheating her. After about a year, she quit her job to take over at home.

The days were full of work. But every evening, as sure as the sun set, David was there. Sometimes he helped her. Sometimes he played with Joey or talked to Harry. But he was there. She could see him out of the corner of her eye as she washed dishes or bent over the steaming clothes iron. And she felt his eyes on her. Now and then they had moments alone, or even a quick walk to get ice cream.

He was still faithful at *shul* and *davened* morning and night, which pleased papa. And he was so gentle with mama. The family talked about their marriage without a word of proposal. They just knew, as Esther and David

53

themselves knew. And everybody but Morris was happy about it.

"A scholar! A presser of pants! Has he no ambition?" Morris's business had grown. He and Sprintzie had a comfortable, even pretentious, home by downtown standards. He was sure she could find another young man, one who would get ahead faster. The streets and shops thronged with East European men who had ventured to America ahead of their sisters and families.

Besides, David had an awful temper. He seemed to live on the edge of frustration. And sometimes the smallest irritation would set him off.

"David," Esther told him after one of his flare-ups, "I don't know if I should marry you. If you'd get as angry with me as I've seen you with others, I think I'd die."

"Why should I ever be angry with you, Esther?" And he looked at her in that tender way that melted her heart.

She knew, though, that she really couldn't change him. She would just have to be careful.

She grinned. "I know. When you get angry with me, just go downstairs and shout at the furnace."

He threw back his head and laughed, in a way he had. "That's no fun!" he said. "The furnace won't talk back."

But neither of them could see anyone else. The two were drawn together—bound together—long before any formal plans were made. Those plans must wait, for mama was far too ill.

More and more mama was confined to her bed. Esther became full-time nurse besides full-time housekeeper, following the doctor's every order and trying to ease her mother's suffering. And as his wife worsened, Israel withdrew. He seemed to turn from life. As other Jews before him, he retreated to the *shul* and hid under his *tallis*.

Two years and ten months after they arrived in Baltimore, Hindl Peltz lay dead, freed from the agony that had wracked her and tortured her loved ones for months.

Observing the custom of centuries, the family arranged for a plain coffin, a common shroud, and a quick burial. Then in the manner of their people, they sat *shivah* for seven days. Mirrors were covered. Family members with shoes removed sat on low boxes about the rooms, while their neighbors and people they knew from factories and stores came to offer condolences and to sit awhile and grieve with them. Then for the rest of thirty days, except for frequent trips to the *shul,* they kept to themselves.

Ceremoniously, at least, their mourning came to an end. But grief, as is its way, refused to obey the calendar. Israel withdrew even more into his religion and prayers. His hair was gray now, his skin wrinkled, and his shoulders rounded. For the first time, he looked his age. He was seventy-two, an old man who seemed to have forgotten his family.

Esther herself grew pale and thin in a kind of physical and emotional crumbling after the ordeal of her mother's illness and death. She had cared for her mother for almost four years, often sensing but rarely admitting that her illness was fatal. This was one fight she had lost. Now she was left with her loss and the realization that if her father's attitude did not change, she would have to assume control again.

At first David grieved with his beloved. Then, when she did not seem to recover, he fretted. One evening he found her slumped at the table, her work only half done, her hair disheveled.

"You can't keep on like this!" He paced nervously, reluctant to confront her, sensitive to her grief.

She shrugged helplessly. "So what can I do?"

He stopped and stood behind her, his hands gripping her shoulders. "Move into my house," he urged. "My mother will take care of you."

She shook her head listlessly.

"And how can I do that? The children—they need me more now than ever."

In her despondency she could not see the relief that had come to the younger ones when their mother's suffering had ended. As far as they were concerned, life was closer to what it should be now than it had been before.

David was beside himself. Would there come no end to her responsibilities—no chance for their life together?

"There's papa," Esther reminded him, her voice a monotonous dirge. "What's to become of him?"

It seemed hopeless.

But because they thought nothing could make things worse, they finally decided to marry, anyway. They reasoned that Esther could still take care of papa and the children.

At first she would permit herself only a small degree of happiness. Were they doing right? Was it good to feel a bit of joy?

Morris, glad to see a break in his sister's depression, went along with their plans and offered his home for both the engagement ceremony and the wedding.

Still Esther couldn't seem to shake off her guilt. Her mother so recently gone, and she should be so happy. When she passed a mirror, she tried not to look at the girl there—who was daily more rounded and glowing. She would compensate for her moments of joy by grieving again or by scolding the children.

"You're so noisy, and your mother, may she rest in peace, not two months in the grave!"

And so they would slink away to be noisy somewhere else.

But as youth and love will do, renewal was not far behind.

One day Esther even stopped at the mirror, admired her flushed cheeks and her shining hair, and said to the image in the glass, "Esther Peltz, you're the luckiest girl in the world!"

Who but David would have waited nearly three years for her? And even yet he was considerate and patient, helping her plan for her family, putting up with her father's moods. *Poor papa!* She almost lapsed into sadness again. Then she told herself, right out loud, what she had been daring to think these past few days.

"Mama would want me to marry. She loved David. She would want me to be happy." She gave herself a tearful smile, then laughed as if she and her mother were sharing her marriage plans.

And maybe they were.

On their wedding day, David and Esther finally knew a day that was completely devoted to them. In true Jewish tradition, they were king and queen.

Esther's dress was the finest white lawn. David's brother Bennie had made it, molded to Esther's figure with scores of tucks that swept from shoulder to hem. She wore a long white veil that was held by a wreath of flowers and greenery. Instead of cutting her hair off to signify the loss of her maidenhood and wearing a *shaytl*, or wig, she had piled her dark curls high on her head to frame the china-doll shape of her face. Surely there was no more elegantly attired bride in Eutaw Place.

And David wore a proper tailor-made suit with a long jacket and boutonniere in the lapel and black patent leather shoes. Their wedding canopy was supported by four slender posts driven in the center of Morris's garden.

Guests arrived in their best, beaming their good

wishes. There would be none of the spirited dancing or a *badchen* to entertain the guests with jokes and mock singing so soon after mama's death. But even Sprintzie had outdone herself in providing a fit feast. Except for missing mama, everything, everything was perfect.

A warm afternoon breeze billowed the white silk of the canopy, reminding everyone of the royalness of the occasion. Surely their home would be the hub, the refuge, the temple that this silk covering suggested.

And when Esther ventured a look at her handsome bridegroom, her joy surged, seeming to stop her very breathing. She would be a good wife, like the rabbi was saying. And now, she felt the ring, warm from David's hand, slip on her finger.

As from far away she heard his firm voice recite the binding words: "Behold, thou art consecrated to me according to the law of Moses and Israel."

How could Esther guess that this fine Jewish scholar would be a blessing to her and her family in a new way—one that would seem strangely alien to her at first.

Then David stooped down, the fragile wine glass from which they had recently sipped in his hand, and Esther heard the crunch under his heel.

As final as this age-old gesture, so final were their vows. As eternal as their people, so was the love that Esther Peltz and David Bronstein would share.

"*Mazel tov! Mazel tov!*" friends and relatives shouted as they showered the couple with kernels of wheat—an explicit hope that God would help them to obey his command to be fruitful and multiply.

ל MESHIACH

THEY LIVED IN AN apartment near her father so Esther could continue to help at home. Ida was in high school now, so she did the cooking with Ruth's help.

But every day Esther took care of her own home and then hurried to her father's. Kosher homes she kept, too, with the complicated process of carefully separating meat and milk, not only in the food she cooked but in the dishes and pans that held it. She did the shopping herself—not trusting Ida to be sure their meat was purchased from the most reliable kosher markets.

And papa, he was still gone a lot. To *shul?* Esther did not know, until one day—reading the Yiddish newspaper—she learned.

"David!" she shouted as she thrust the newspaper at him. Amidst the list of marriage licenses issued were the names of Israel Peltz and a woman Esther only slightly remembered from the synagogue.

"How can he do this, with mama gone only a few months!" Esther wept her hurt and disappointment.

"Nu, nu! Maybe it's for the best. Your papa has been very lonely. She can keep house for him and take care of the children."

Esther did not want anybody else taking care of her brothers and sisters. "How can he? How can he?" she kept repeating.

But he did. A few days later the new Mrs. Peltz and her two grown sons moved in.

It was a disaster from the beginning. The children resented her, and she had little patience with them. In the synagogue other men reproached Israel about his new sons. "They're not mine," he retorted. "They're hers."

Almost as quickly as it had begun, the marriage was over, adding to Israel Peltz's bitterness. Nothing had gone well for him since they had come to America.

So they settled again into their old routine with Ida able to carry on at home more and more. And it was well. For Esther was pregnant, and the two households were almost more than even her vigor could bear.

And David—he worked. Where others slacked off at the shop, David would pick up an extra bundle of clothes and make a few more dollars. Sometimes his regular eight dollars a week increased to eighteen. They were saving, and they were happy.

But marriage hadn't improved his temper . . . like the time he arrived home after twelve hours at the shop. Esther saw him coming a half block away. There she was, gossiping on the porch with Mrs. Schwartz, and his supper not ready. She scurried up the steps as fast as her cumbersome body would let her—but not fast enough. She was still breathless and very busy at the stove when she heard David open the door and felt his eyes boring her back.

"Well!"

She turned defiantly. "So I sat down to visit with my good neighbor for a few minutes. That's a crime?"

"I'm hungry."

She slammed the pans, angry with herself, furious with him. *Why?* She didn't know except that the child was heavy in her; and she was hot and weary, and he had no right. . . !

"*Oh-oy-oy!*" he moaned and, in a way he had, beat the side of his head with his hand. "What have I married?"

"What have *I* married? A crazy man?"

And all that evening they glowered at one another and then crept in on far sides of the bed.

Only when he was asleep did Esther permit a tear to escape. Poor fellow—he worked so hard! She should have had his supper ready. She turned clumsily, the child keeping her awake. She had noticed that he had been even more tired and anxious lately.

And he no longer *davened* or seemed to care that she kept a kosher home and lighted the *Shabbes* candles. He was too tired or too busy to go to *shul*, so she went with her father. Marriage wasn't at all as she had imagined it. Where was the sensitive scholar she had first loved? Buried in the drudgery of that miserable tailor shop, that's where. Worried about her and the baby. Putting up with her and her family. But she loved him—she loved him so. For at least two weeks his supper was ready on time every evening.

It was two o'clock one night when the baby announced his coming. Esther laughed at David's nervousness,

61

watching him step into his trousers backward.

"It will be hours!" she said, but something about the next contraction made her wonder.

The nurse David brought walked into the room and immediately sent him running for the doctor. But he arrived to find a fourteen-pound boy wrapped and cradled in the arms of a happy mother—who was obviously enjoying the joke she had played on them.

They called him Morris. And by nightfall both clans had visited and agreed he was the most beautiful baby in all of Baltimore.

While none of the younger members of the family observed their other duties as Jews, still the baby must be ushered into the family of Israel properly. On the eighth day they gathered to celebrate the circumcision.

Esther, still in bed, listened only during the initial prayer of the circumciser. Then she pulled a pillow close over her head so she could not hear her son's cries.

Afterward, while she nursed and comforted him, the family enjoyed wine and sponge cake, united for this little time in the faith of their fathers.

Household routine soon found a steady track again. David's temper did not flare so often now, but he brooded. And to Esther, that was even worse.

"Why don't you get another job, David? You don't like working in the tailor shop."

"What can I do? I don't know enough English to get a better job."

Esther pretended ignorance. But she had seen some clippings from an English newspaper under their dresser scarf. She didn't have to read English to understand the picture of a streetcar and the familiar words, "Help Wanted."

"You could be a streetcar motorman, maybe? That pays more."

She couldn't suppress the twinkle in her eyes when he looked at her suspiciously. And they laughed together and agreed that yes, he should take English lessons again.

So David and Harry decided to begin again at Eutaw Place. In fact, Jacob was already going there a couple of evenings a week, and he had great things to say about a new teacher.

At first, it was only two nights a week. In between, David studied.

"Why don't you go more often, David? Then you'll learn faster," Esther suggested and then wished she had not been so generous with their time together.

So four evenings a week he swallowed a quick supper and ran to swing aboard the trolley that took him to the Baptist church.

Harry wasn't the tenacious sort. And Jacob, too, began missing classes, but David hung on. Esther, busy with her baby and home, didn't really mind his going. But she was irritated when he seemed so absorbed the few evenings he was home. She understood his need to study. But even when he wasn't in his books, his eyes had a faraway look. Sometimes, she had to speak several times to make him hear. Almost always now she lit the *Shabbes* candles alone.

David had found the Eutaw Place Baptist Church just as he remembered. But lessons were different now. He had picked up some English on his own, and there was Miss Gaither, the new teacher.

Ruby Gaither had a serious way about her—she was very much the old maid, David decided, but she was fun, too. And something else. After a half hour with an English grammar and reading book, she opened the Bible—the *Tenach,* which he had been neglecting these long months—and they read the Scripture in English together. He stumbled along, resorting to his Hebrew-English dictionary but growing more confident with each lesson.

Even in English, the words were beautiful. Not like the Hebrew, of course, but he could see that Ruby Gaither loved the Holy Scripture as much as he ever had.

And often as they studied—she didn't have to tell him he could see for himself—the *Meshiach* they read about described the Jesus she worshiped. Sometimes she would show him the very same text he was reading in a New Testament she kept beside her. Faithful Jews had followed this Jesus, and part of their testimony to the world was how the Old Testament prophecies had been fulfilled. The predictions he knew by heart seemed to be fulfilled in the life of this man the Christians worshiped.

Slowly he even began to see Jesus' presence in the Old Testament. As they were reading the familiar words of Genesis 1, David suddenly noticed that God had said, "Let *us* make man in *our* image, after *our* likeness."

And there was the man who appeared with Shadrach, Meshach, and Abednego in the fiery furnace. Even King Nebuchadnezzar had said "the fourth is like a son of the gods." Could that have been Jesus of Nazareth?

Yet, just when he would think that, David could see the icons, the crucifix, and the crowds shouting, "Beat the *Zhid!* Beat the *Zhid!*" as they descended on him with stones and clubs.

So when their reading or conversation threatened, David brought up a point of grammar he couldn't understand or remembered that Esther was waiting for him.

As the classes dwindled, they decided to move from the drafty church to the comfort of Ruby's home, which she shared with another teacher and a nurse. There, four evenings a week, the three women provided a plate of cookies or a fresh-baked cake to sweeten their studies. So kind they were, so full of faith in the strange man they called "Christ," that David came to trust and respect them. And he saw that what they believed made a difference in their lives and attitudes.

Often, now, the New Testament became as much a textbook as the Old. As he read he realized that it was not a strange, alien book but one that echoed the words of the Jewish prophets and the writings of the Torah over and over again. This Jesus was a Jew who lived by the Holy Word, one who let that Word guide everything he did.

Then one day when they were reading Isaiah 53, David suddenly realized that the *Meshiach* described there—despised and rejected by men—was the Christ crucified on Calvary. And he had died because "it was the will of the Lord to bruise him . . . so that by his stripes" man would be healed.

No longer did he have to feel guilty about the death of Jesus. No longer could the accusing words, "Beat the Jews, the Christ-killers!" ring in his ears. Jesus Christ had died to save mankind; it was God's will.

After that, each word David read seemed to speak to him. But he could not face the conviction that grew within him. For it threatened everything he held dear—his wife, his family, and his religion.

Each evening after they had tired of reading, Ruby Gaither and David talked a while. Usually these discussions were as casual as their conversation began one particular Saturday afternoon.

"How is little Morris, David?" she inquired.

"Not so little! He's nearly six months old now and a real load for Esther to carry."

"And your work?"

"As tiresome as ever." Suddenly David felt he could confide what he had not yet had the courage to tell

Esther. "You know the motorman's job?"

Miss Gaither nodded. They had discussed his dream before.

"I don't qualify. I'm not tall enough." His words came out in an explosion, even though he tried to hold back his pent-up anger. Was he doomed to life in a tailor shop because he lacked an inch of the required five-feet-ten? He swallowed hard.

"What's the use of my learning English?"

But she did not reply.

"Well, why should I try? I might as well be in the *shtetl!*"

She raised her eyes to meet his. "David?"

Something like tears rose to choke him. Why did she have to be so kind?

"David, it isn't only English you have been learning here. You are seeing things in the Bible that you never saw before."

David stared intently at the chocolate cake.

"You are finding your Messiah in the New Testament."

He looked up. He wanted to speak, but he only nodded dumbly.

"Shall we pray together?"

"I . . . can only pray in Hebrew," he stammered. "The English doesn't come that well."

Miss Gaither smiled. "I'm sure he understands Hebrew."

In years to come, David did not remember just what he had said. But such was the intensity of his prayer, such the struggle of his heart and mind, that his shirt was wet with perspiration.

He left without another word. At home, he could not speak to Esther; he could not sleep. As his mind went over the passages Ruby Gaither had showed him, he became filled with the same fervor and longing he had felt as they prayed together. What he had been reading had spoken to him personally, and he believed. There was no use denying it.

Early that morning before Esther awoke, David addressed an envelope to Miss Gaither and wrote in his uncertain English, "I believe Jesus is my Messiah."

Something happened when he sealed that letter. Something he could not explain. The streetcar sang a song on the rails. The tailor shop became a corner of heaven. Even at the close of a long day, the steps to their flat seemed a ladder of prayer, and Esther and Morris were surrounded with a rosy glow. Supper wasn't ready. But he laughed and kissed his wife.

"Are you crazy?" Esther sidled around looking at him curiously as he played with the baby.

He must tell her! They could not remain close with such a secret between them.

But not yet. She was very firm in her mind, and she knew nothing good about Jesus. She wasn't ready. Nor was he. First he must learn more so he could show her plainly. So he waited, studying, storing up what he would need to convince his strong-willed wife that Jesus was the Messiah.

# MESHUMAD!

DAVID WAS HOME more now, and for that Esther was glad. But was he really there? He sat with his book, this English book that looked like a Bible, and read and read—until she sometimes wanted to scream.

Had it been wise to agree that he should return to his English studies? This change seemed to occur after that. And didn't his knowledge of English put a barrier between them? She couldn't read the English words he was reading now. Maybe she would never learn, at least not until she could speak the language better.

Then, one night, he told her.

"Esther, I have found the Messiah."

"All our rabbis have been looking for *Meshiach,* and *you*

have found him?" she replied suspiciously.

"Yes, here in this book. He is Jesus of Nazareth: *Yeshua.*"

Esther recoiled at the hated name that had spelled death to her people for centuries.

"I believe he is God's Son, our Savior, and I want you to believe in him, too," he replied in a voice she thought too calm, too soft, and much too confident—as if he didn't have to defend himself, because what he said was true.

"Never! Never!" She ran from him to her only refuge: her Jewish baby boy. Circumcised. Prayed over each time she lighted the *Shabbes* candles or placed him in his crib.

When David went to work the next day, she bundled little Morris up and ran to Mrs. Schwartz.

"My David has turned *goy!*"

"You must be wrong. David is an educated man. He would not believe such rubbish!"

"But it's true!" Tears she had held back rushed out in a wailing that had annoyed her when her mother had cried that way.

"What will father think? And Morris? A *meshumad*—a willing convert—in the family!" She pronounced the word with all the hatred of the ages—the hatred of those who had been forced to become Christians by threats of death or torture, of those who had died, and those who lived in constant resistance.

"He will disgrace us all!" She clung to her friend, weeping tears of anger and confusion.

Mrs. Schwartz stroked her hair and held her close. The older women muttered words of condolence. "Now, Esther, don't be so upset." But she could not hide her own horror at what had happened. "Perhaps he can be changed," she said, voicing the only possible solution. "Why don't you talk to your father about it?"

That Saturday night, Esther had her defense ready:

David's father and her own. These formidable sons of the Covenant came prepared with their best. But David's new faith outshone all their arguments.

With his Hebrew New Testament he showed them where one prophecy after the other was fulfilled in *Yeshua,* until even these men retreated to their authority as fathers—admonishing him to consider carefully the step he was taking.

Esther listened. She was not learned enough to understand half of what they said. And even though her whole being sided with the faith of her fathers, she was proud of David. He was so sure of himself. Never once did he lose his temper or raise his voice.

But he was wrong. And she knew it.

All her long-restrained anger at his neglect and preoccupation rose to her consciousness. And deep below that was a horror inspired by years of suffering in the *shtetl.* The Jewishness within her—carefully traced back to the twelve sons of Jacob—was as much a part of her as the color of her hair. How had he wrenched himself from it? Such a change seemed impossible!

When next she saw him reading his New Testament, she jerked it from his hands, tore it with strength she did not know she had, and threw it in his face.

But although he was obviously hurt and worried by her outburst, David calmly retrieved the pieces. And the next day, he had another. Her violence had accomplished nothing. Her good sense and frugality told her it wouldn't do any good to destroy the new one; he would only buy another. Instead she hurled the ultimate threat at him. "I will leave you. I will divorce you." She spoke the words slowly to convey the days of thought that had gone into them.

The look he turned on her revealed his panic, yet he would not fight. That she could have endured; there was some hope in arguing. But with David, there seemed to be only one answer. An answer she would not accept.

When she was alone, she cried. Why did this have to come between them? She thought she had found security, someone to love and care for her. Now he had deserted her for this Jesus.

Again she went to Mrs. Schwartz. But the poor woman was in over her head. "You should see the rabbi, Esther. I have never had such a problem, and I don't know how to advise you."

Of course the rabbi had been told of David's apostasy. But he heard Esther out. Yes, she had cause for divorce. She should, in fact, divorce him. But first she must have proof.

"Go with him sometime. See where he goes and what he does. See for sure that it is a Christian church and that the *goyim* regard him as a Christian."

Could she? Would she dare? She would so she could divorce him, if all else failed.

One night she surprised him by asking if she could go with him. Mrs. Schwartz would keep Morris, who was now old enough to walk and a bother when he was forced to sit still or keep quiet.

They rode the streetcar to Eutaw Place and joined those who moved toward the Baptist church. Esther scanned the crowd nervously. There were many other Jews. Also many *goyim*. Why had she come? At the door she almost turned back, but David tugged on her arm.

Once inside, she looked about. No crucifix? No icons? No bowing and chanting? This could have been a synagogue, so plain were the walls, so simple the furnishings. Not at all as she had pictured a church. She relaxed ever so slightly.

They sang hymns in English, her David as heartily as the next. Then the speaker was introduced: Dr. Arno

Gaebelein, a little man with a goatee who looked more like a Jew than a Gentile.

He might have been speaking right to her, especially since David had brought her so close to the front. He talked about *Yeshua*, showing again and again, just as David had done, that Jesus was the Messiah her people had waited for. As he preached, Esther kept feeling, *That's mine. That's Jewish; it belongs to me. But why does he say it? He's a* goy. Soon her head was pounding so hard that she held it in her hands and wept.

Finally she heard Dr. Gaebelein end with a closing prayer, addressing it to the God of Abraham, Isaac, and Jacob.

David's patient witness and prayer reached their climax in Esther that moment. She prayed to the God she knew and trusted.

O Lord, help me know if this place is right! If this man is right! If David is right! Help me know if Yeshua *is the Messiah!*

Afterward, David's friends crowded about her and with a pride she couldn't help but notice he introduced her. "This is Esther, my wife." There was one special introduction, one that Esther recoiled from.

"Esther, this is Miss Gaither, my English teacher."

David's teacher. The hated one who had drawn him astray. Esther tensed, but Ruby Gaither walked the few steps between them and drew Esther into her arms like a sister. "I'm so happy to meet you, Esther."

Somehow the love in her voice and her manner reached out to Esther, no matter how hard she tried to withdraw from it. No other Gentile had ever reached out to her in love.

"May I come and visit you?" she asked.

Esther heard herself consenting.

When Ruby Gaither climbed the steps to their little flat the next week, she had a teddy bear for Morris and a warm embrace for Esther. Slowly she shared the story of David's search, and as she talked about the passages that had influenced him, Esther began to be interested.

Maybe she started reading the Bible because she didn't want to be left out of something that was so important to her husband. Maybe she was a little jealous that David had shared so much with someone else. She was not sure.

But after Miss Gaither left, Esther found David's Hebrew New Testament and began to read. Because her Hebrew was not good enough, she bought a Yiddish Bible. Slowly she began to read both the New Testament and the Old.

She read when she should have been washing clothes. She read when she should have been cooking supper. But she was careful to hide her Bible when David was around.

And every day her wonder grew. Jesus, whom she had hated and feared, was himself a Jew—and a good one. He had never deserted his faith. And he never did anything but good. He even died—for her and her people, the Bible said.

One day she was studying the New Testament when she felt a longing for the familiar words of the Psalms.

Quickly she flipped the pages back to the writings of David. As she looked at the page, one verse caught her eyes: "Be still, and know that I am God."

Was David's Jesus, *Yeshua*, speaking to her? The thought reverberated through her mind as she returned to the passages David and Miss Gaither had been showing her. Flipping back and forth from the New Testament to the Old, she suddenly knew that David was right.

That night when she heard his step on the stairs, she did not hide her Bible. As he entered the door she confessed, tears streaming down her face.

"David, I have found the Messiah. I believe!"

7 "HE THAT LOVETH"

ESTHER KEPT HER BELIEF a secret. No one but David, Miss Gaither, and the Christians at Eutaw Baptist knew. The New Testament, however, was no longer a hidden book in the David Bronstein home. They attended every meeting of Christians they could without attracting attention. And Ruby Gaither was drawn into the family as a teacher and friend.

Esther knew she should tell her father, but she was afraid he would disown her. Both families were already upset about David's apostasy—a furor she had helped inspire.

And then Ruby Gaither suggested that Jacob come to

stay with her and the two other women with whom she shared her home. Ruby had been helping Jacob with his English so he could reenter school and complete what he had lost when his father had persuaded him to sell newspapers full-time. But the trolley ride home every evening had soon become too tiring, keeping the fifteen-year-old boy out late into the night. So Ruby suggested that he help them with the chores to earn his keep, and she would make sure he went back to school.

The prospect of Jacob's leaving home channeled the family's frustration toward an outsider—Ruby Gaither.

"Jacob will not live with those proselytizing females," Morris stormed. But Morris was no paragon of Hebrew devotion himself, and everyone knew it. His communication with the God of Abraham, Isaac, and Jacob had long ago given way to a merchant's haggling and conniving. Esther held firmly to her conviction that going to Miss Gaither's would keep Jacob off the streets and out of the sweatshop. But still Israel Peltz wavered.

Then Jacob came home one day feverish and complaining of a sore throat. To Esther, it seemed as if God had taken the matter into his own hands. For when Jacob was examined by doctors at the nearby Johns Hopkins Hospital, they found a spot on his lung as well as a severe case of tonsillitis, which they immediately operated on. Then they recommended rest and care in the country. Ruby Gaither's home was the only choice the family had.

Ever since the relatives had learned of David's apostasy, they had come to visit every Saturday night. Sometimes they would play cards, and sometimes they would talk about the Talmud and the Holy Books. Quietly, without direct pressure, they were trying to cajole David back into the faith of their fathers. And David was gently attempting to persuade them. His strong bent to scholarships and his knowledge of the Holy Books insured him a respectful hearing.

One Thursday evening when Esther was out shopping, someone knocked at the door.

The family's concern must be increasing, David thought as he opened the door to see Esther's oldest brother standing there.

For a while Morris attempted amiable conversation. But not long, for Morris conducted everything as he did his business—in a brief, curt, and often unpleasant manner.

"So you went and smeared yourself," he said finally, his face twisted in anger.

David could not mistake the tone of his voice or the implication of complete disgrace. Yet he was not going to lose his temper. He was determined to approach Morris as quietly as he had the others, though not with Scripture.

Slowly David began to tell him how he had begun to feel that the rituals they performed each day had little meaning.

"The rabbis in Eastern Europe ignored theology, the reasons behind our rituals. You know that, Morris. You felt disillusioned long before I did."

"Not I." Morris's defiance seemed to increase. "Don't compare yourself to me, you *meshumad!*"

David knew his brother-in-law would not let him change the subject, so he continued even though Morris's face quivered with emotion.

"Once I asked myself the simple question, Why? I knew that all I had was a collection of habits. But I continued to observe them . . . until I began to take English lessons at Eutaw Baptist. Slowly the familiar passages of the Tenach came alive again. Only now I was reading them from an English Bible, and they were leading me to the Messiah, Jesus of Nazareth."

Morris jerked at the hated name.

"Don't talk to me about your Jesus," he screamed. "You're crazy, David. But why be so open about it? You can still attend the synagogue. Nobody would have to know the difference."

"I can't do that, Morris."

Suddenly the man lunged toward David, slapping him across the face with a swift, hard blow that knocked him back in his chair.

For a moment the two stared at one another. David would not respond to the assault, and Morris seemed to be waiting for some provocation before he continued. When none came, he turned and walked out of the house, slamming the door behind him.

David sat there stunned. *Who is he to come and rule my family?* Finally he opened the door and ran out onto the sidewalk.

"If you ever come again, I'll break your neck" he shouted. "Don't you dare come back. You're nobody."

Morris did not turn around, but David knew he had heard him by the way his step quickened. *He won't fight here in the street,* David thought, *not Morris Peltz, the respectable furrier.* How ironic that their firstborn son should be named for this man!

When Esther returned later that evening, David and Ruby Gaither were sitting, talking. Esther could tell Ruby had been crying.

"Morris will make Jacob come back home. I know he will," Ruby was saying as Esther entered the room, her arms full of groceries.

But Morris never had that chance. The next evening he left home for the synagogue but hurried instead—as he had for many other Fridays—to the room above his

ESTHER

shop. He was late, and the other men had been waiting, so he quickly opened the street door, leaving his key in the lock.

When the night watchman found it, he called Morris's home. And Morris's wife, Sprintzie, called the police. For several weeks she had suspected that Morris was going to the shop on holy days, gambling with his friends in the room upstairs rather than attending synagogue.

No sooner had Sprintzie hung up the phone than she regretted it. What had she done to her husband's reputation as a businessman? Quickly she hurried over to join the police at Morris's store.

It was Sprintzie who diverted the officer—"Not over here, upstairs!" she said—when he came close to finding Morris and his friends hiding in the downstairs of the shop. The danger passed.

But now she was threatening to tell everyone at the synagogue that "Morris, the big-shot furrier, plays cards on a holy day." Morris's renewed arguments about Jacob were lost in his defense of himself and his efforts to redeem his standing with the family.

Israel Peltz remained helpless amidst the emotions swirling around him. Puzzled by the change in his children, impressed by David's scholarly presentation, still he was only torn—neither convinced that David was right nor that he should be censured. Still Morris and his accusations didn't particularly disturb him, for Israel knew that David was a better Jew than Morris.

A pitiful man, Israel Peltz. In his prime he had flourished as the unquestioned head of a large family, the owner of a prosperous business, a leader in *shul*. Change had come too fast and too late. Removed from his environment, shaken by the death of his wife and his disastrous remarriage, and now confronted by his divided family—he only retreated further into *shul* life. But even as he prayed, he was riddled by the questions that David aroused.

Meanwhile, Esther and David continued their witness and learning. They bought a home, studied toward naturalization, and saved their money. As much a student as ever, David stayed out of his wife's way while she ran the home and managed their finances.

Morris was a mischievous, healthy two year old. And Esther was pregnant again. She shone with the satisfaction of one who has her house in order. The strength and ingenuity that had brought her family out of Russia stayed by her now as she became the maternal leader of the extended family—but not without opposition from Sprintzie.

Then slowly she began to see a subtle change in David. Like a restlessness, it was; long hours at work and study and good Jewish food—which in Esther's Yiddish heart should cure every ill—could not assuage it.

"I want to go to school, Esther," he finally confessed.

"But you already know so much! You should want to learn more?"

"I believe God wants me to be a missionary to our people. For that I must have education."

"And aren't you already telling your family about *Meshiach?*" she persisted.

David shook his head. "It isn't enough. I have so much to learn!"

Well, maybe it would pass, like a spell of indigestion, Esther reasoned.

David struggled with this new conflict. Why couldn't he be content? He was making a good living. He had peace at home and fellowship with other Christians. Was this urgency in him what Ruby Gaither termed a "call"?

Whatever it was, he spent restless nights in inner conflict and prayer.

But he couldn't go to a school for missionaries until he had a high-school diploma. How far would his education in Russia count toward that? He had no way of knowing. And besides, he had responsibilities—a wife and soon two children.

He might have given up, except that one day he happened into the bookstore whose proprietor had first sent him to the English school at Eutaw Place.

"Quite a studier, aren't you?" The man chatted as he wrapped David's purchase. "A fellow about your age with the same yen for learning was in the other day. He's going to an academy in Pennsylvania."

David's hand stopped midway in its plunge into his pocket for change.

"He said there's even a Hebrew-Christian going there, preparing to be a minister," the man continued as he handed the package to David.

"But . . . how can a man go to school and earn a living for his wife and family?"

"This man is doing it. Has a tailor shop. You interested?"

"Very much!" David's hand trembled as he laid his coins on the counter.

"Well, the next time he comes in I'll ask him for more information. He might even help you get a job. If you're sure you're interested, that is. I wouldn't want to put him to a lot of trouble for nothing."

"I sure am," David assured the man. "Just find out for me! . . . And thanks!"

Turning toward home, David felt light-headed. Other men were going to school and supporting a family. Surely, God could work it out for him, too. He scarcely saw the crowd that hurried about him as he maneuvered along the sidewalk. Then he thought of Esther, and his steps lagged. Maybe he shouldn't tell her. No, he couldn't threaten their new closeness; she should know. But she would object—of that he was sure.

Which she did. And more so as he made contact with Gettysburg Academy and prepared to go. Leaving would mean deserting her family. Ida and Ruth, who had been going to a local mission's story-telling hour, had only needed David's added testimony to become Christians; now they would be left alone with their father, who had no idea of their conversion. And Joey? There was the hurt. Only recently her nine-year-old brother had been selling newspapers, and a car had run over his foot, cutting off one of his toes. Israel Peltz had been so upset that he had decided Joey must go into one of the United Hebrew Charities' new homes for orphans.

Esther had not carried her baby brother all the way from Nikolayev to have him end up an orphan. The maternal instincts inherited from centuries of *shtetl* Jews who had cared for their own revolted against it.

But what was she to do? She had a child of her own and a husband who wanted to go back to school as if he were her younger brother. She believed that part of her purpose in life had been completed when she was converted: she had found the Messiah—her Savior.

But now she realized that he beckoned toward a second purpose: service. Service to him. Then to her husband and family. And finally to those around her. She had cared for her mother's and father's children since she was twelve; now she must care for her own.

But now she must tell Morris and her father that she, too, was a Christian. She had listened to their cries of "Divorce him," she had attempted to smooth over their hatred and disgust, and she had listened as David had tried to tell them why he believed as he did. Now that

David would dedicate his life to missionary work, Esther had no choice.

She waited until a family gathering at Morris's. She and David had patched up their initial difficulties with him, and they had seen him and Sprintzie occasionally. They had been pleased to be included in this party, and now they must ruin what little progress they had made.

After dinner, when the men had gathered for their usual discussions, David began.

"I have decided to go back to school so I can be trained to tell our people about the Messiah."

The look on her brother's face told Esther that he could not believe—would not listen—to what David was saying. Not only had his brother-in-law rejected their faith; now he wanted to denounce that faith publicly before his own people.

"Traitor!"

Morris's voice was louder, his reaction quicker than Esther's father's, but one echoed the other.

She must speak!

"I believe in Jesus Christ, too," she said, not loudly. But the meaning of her words quieted the noise around her. Everyone in the room—Sprintzie, Ida, Ruth, Jacob, and finally her father and Morris turned toward her. Sprintzie began to scream, "What kind of a family is this? All turned *goyim*, all *meshumad!*"

But Morris and Israel Peltz just looked at Esther, unable to speak. Then with a soft hacking cry, Esther's father hid his face in his hands, sobbing out his sorrow at all that had happened since he had left his homeland.

Esther knelt beside him and tried to put her arm on his shoulder, but he shook himself free and turned to face her.

"Go, Esther. You are no longer a member of this family," he cried, all the defiance and anger of the last years in the finality of those words. "No one shall speak of you or your husband or your family as long as I live. . . . You are lost to us. *Mechuleh!*"

For the past months, Esther had been preparing herself for her father's rejection. She had cried one day not too long ago when she had read Jesus' words in Matthew 11, "For I am come to set a man at variance against his father, and the daughter against her mother."

And for weeks now she had held on to his admonition "He that loveth father or mother . . . son or daughter . . . more than me is not worthy of me."

But now all she had dreaded became a reality. For when Israel Peltz spoke the word *mechuleh,* he cut her off, not only from himself, but from the brothers and sisters she had raised as sons and daughters. It would be years before she would see her father again.

GETTYSBURG ACADEMY

HANNAH WAS BORN in January of 1912. Esther cried as she held the baby in her arms, for the child symbolized all she had lost and all she had gained.

In February Esther and David received their naturalization. And by late summer they had rented their Baltimore home and were on their way to Gettysburg, Pennsylvania.

Gettysburg, a town rich in history, traditions, and educational institutions, edged over a bit to make room for these transients of a different brand, while the Jewish students and their families drew together to share their Jewishness.

Instructors at the academy were willing to do the necessary juggling so David could earn the high-school credits he needed, and soon David, Esther, three-and one-half-year-old Morris, and nine-month-old Hannah were settled in a small house. David found work for a tailor—low-skilled work, basting in the fine skirt pleats that were then in style. But it was work he could do at home in spare hours and Esther could help him by hemming the skirts and sewing hooks and eyes on the plackets. With their earnings, their savings, and rent money from their Baltimore house, they were able to survive.

Again they were curiosities—Hebrews in a Gentile Christian church. After living in the Jewish ghettos of Russia and Baltimore, being one of only seven Jewish families in town took some getting used to.

The Bronsteins' new faith in a Messiah who had already come did not separate them from the other Jews. Esther kept a kosher home. The other students' Old World faith had suffered so in their Americanization that to be kosher was enough. The Bronsteins' attendance at a Christian church only brought some good-natured kidding; they were Jews together.

Still there were times when the other Jews would question them, if not out of curiosity more than anything else. Often these questions came when she and the other women went walking on Saturdays.

"A nice Jewish woman like you," someone would say. "Why do you believe in Jesus?"

"You don't understand," she would begin. "Jesus doesn't belong to the Gentiles. He came to us, and as a nation we didn't accept him. But individuals did. The first Christian church was all Jewish—every one of them."

Esther did not prolong the conversation. For one thing, she wasn't ready to convert others. She was still searching herself. But she answered their questions, and one day even confided what bothered her most.

"When I go into a Christian church, I see a room full of nice people, *fayner goyim*. But we Jews are smart, too. Why didn't we accept him? . . . Why won't we now?" She paused to control her voice and her emotions. She didn't want to offend her friends; she loved them.

Then she added, "Why don't we become complete Jews? We are not complete without Jesus, without our Messiah!"

Always after their questions and her answers were over, she would pray silently, *Help remove their veils so they can see that* Yeshua *is our Messiah. Then when he comes back, he will be King of Kings and Lord of Lords, to Jew and Gentile. And we will all be one people, belonging to the Jewish Messiah.*

Esther was lucky that these early Jewish acquaintances were so accepting. Later she would know the pain of rejection.

David would earn his diploma in two years, but they both knew this was not the end. To be a missionary he must have more schooling. Where? Homesick, worried about her family, Esther fervently prayed it would be in Baltimore. But David had heard of a school in Chicago that specialized in training for practical Christian work: Moody Bible Institute.

"Chicago! You should go so far away?"

"The Chicago school is a good one, and tuition is free."

"Free?" Esther's managing mind computed this advantage. "But Chicago is big and dirty. And so far! How would we live?"

She already knew what his answer would be: "God will provide." She believed that, too. In fact she enjoyed the adventure of watching just how God might do that, knowing that David's own skilled hands would help the Lord along.

David softened at her smile. "We'll go back to Baltimore first, my *meydl*. You shall see that Ida and Ruth and Jacob are all right."

Esther's interest in her family was not only that they be cared for, though in her heart the younger ones were always *"mein kinder."* Her greatest concern was that they come to know the Messiah.

Esther could never forget the shock she had felt when she had first studied the Bible and seen the passage "He that believeth on him is not condemned: but he that believeth not is condemned already, because he hath not believed in the name of the only begotten Son of God."

Suddenly she thought of her mother. Would she go to hell? Surely not. Still . . .

She had gone back to the crippled woman at the mission where she had bought her Yiddish Bible. But when Esther had explained her problem and asked, "Is my mother in hell?" the woman had replied, "What does the Bible say?" She showed Esther the same passage, acknowledging its truth.

Esther had grabbed the Bible from her, saying, "I could spit in your face. But I'm a good Jewish woman, and they don't do that."

She had stood there holding her Bible and shaking. "You should tell me that my mother's in hell. You don't hold a candle to her."

Later she had asked Ruby Gaither the same question.

"Did anyone ever tell her about Jesus?" Ruby had asked.

"No," Esther replied.

"Then why should I judge your mother? Let's leave her in the hands of God. . . . If she never heard about Jesus, and she believed in God, let him judge her. I won't assign her to hell."

Esther had been comforted by Ruby's reply, but she

had never lost a bit of that fear. The rest of her family was still alive, and somehow she would reach them. Daily she prayed for them. She knew Jacob's faith was growing from his and Ruby's letters. And Ruth and Ida were already Christians. But there was her father and Harry, who was married now and doing well in the grocery business in Florida. And what about Morris?

Still, it was Joseph who tore at her heart. Joey, now eleven, was still in an orphanage. Would he ever be reunited with his family? She wondered if it was right to leave them all to go about telling others of the Messiah?

For now a visit would have to do and after that Chicago.

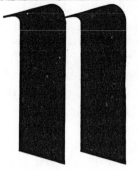

A MAN FULLY CONSECRATED

AGAIN ESTHER WAS ABOARD a lurching, screeching train, approaching a great city through miles of switches and a tangle of track. A gray haze hovered in the hot, August air, and in that haze was the penetrating smell of cattle yards. Endless rows of back porches—hung with drying clothes, gray as the sooty air and overrun with ragged children—rimmed the tracks. Compared to Chicago, the Baltimore train yards had been a garden.

But that was long ago. Now she was nine years older and had a husband—such a wonderful husband!—and children of her own. Seventeen-year-old Ida had decided to come with them to Chicago, leaving only Ruth at home with Esther's father. *Someday he will forgive me,*

Esther thought as the train approached their destination.

Ida pointed out anything that would interest the wriggling Morris as Esther began to rouse two- and one-half-year-old Hannah. What awaited them here? They had nothing but their savings—helped by the sale of their home and furnishings in Baltimore, their youth, and the promise of God's help. Surely David's acceptance at Moody was a sign of his direction.

More twistings, grindings, more acrid smoke, and the windows became black mirrors as the train edged into the underground tunnel near the station. This time there would be no welcoming brothers and father. She tried to remind herself of God's help, but she was frightened. Where would they turn? What was the first thing they should do?

Once inside the great, cavernous depot they saw a sign over the heads of the crowd: "Moody Bible Institute."

The sign was familiar to trainmen and depot attendants. More than fourteen hundred students were expected to arrive that fall, and older students were on hand to guide the newcomers who arrived on every train.

Since its opening in 1889, Moody Bible Institute had made an impression on the city of Chicago, one that seemed too unlikely to be believable. That one man, fired by God, could raise such a center of Christian influence and teaching was still a wonder, even in this blustering, can-do city. The Chicago man on the street had heard vaguely about thousands of Moody graduates already on the worldwide mission field or pastoring churches all across America. That reputation had brought David here.

Soon he was to learn much more about the great figures who headed the school at this time: Dr. R. A. Torrey, president; Dr. James M. Gray, dean; Dr. C. I. Scofield, Henry Parsons Crowell, and William R. Newell.

David would find a great inspiration there—perhaps the greatest in the heritage left by Moody, who as a young man had heard the challenge, "The world has yet to see what God will do with a man fully consecrated to him."

But this reinforcement was in the future—all unknown to the young Jews who left the train that torrid August morning. Meanwhile, it was comfort enough to have help in finding a couple of cabs and to have a note to give the driver, describing the route to their destination.

So arriving wasn't half so hard. When they reached the tall, red-brick buildings on LaSalle Street, they learned that the school had no housing for married students. But a kind assistant in the office told them of a furnished basement apartment about three blocks from the school. God—and his people—were taking care of them, Esther reassured herself. Yet her steps were heavy and slow as she and Ida with the two little ones trudged down the hot cement walk toward their new home. For David had dismissed one cab in the interest of economy.

Yet it felt good to walk again, after two days on the train. She glanced at Ida, fresh and eager in this adventure. Yes, it was good to have her there. As the children skipped and played, Esther began to look about, curious at what her neighborhood was like.

Mr. Moody had built his school on the north side of town in an area that, less than forty years before, had been leveled by the Great Chicago Fire. Now it had been rebuilt with row after row of monotonous, narrow brick houses, much as in Baltimore. Shops of every kind occupied the first floors, and narrow, litter-strewn alleyways separated the buildings. Ten or twelve steps led directly from the sidewalk to a porch and entrance that she supposed opened onto the two or three upper floors. On the side of each porch, another four or five steps led down to the lower apartments.

ESTHER

Children were everywhere, some even playing ball in the streets, dodging horse-drawn traffic and the sparking, squealing trolley cars. Women and a few old men lounged on the steps, escaping what must be the unbearable heat of the apartments. Some glanced at them curiously but showed little interest. Then they were "home," arriving just as David dismissed the driver, whose tired horse pulled the empty cab away.

Only three weeks had passed. Already, Esther was settled in. Ida had found work. David was deep in his schoolwork, which consisted mostly of Bible studies, more studies in English and rhetoric, and missionary courses. That David! Could he never learn enough? He was at once a pride and a pain to her.

One day nineteen-year-old Jacob knocked at the door. Dejected, confused, he told his story slowly, a story they had suspected during their brief stay in Baltimore.

Jacob had fallen in love with Ruby Gaither, who was fifteen years older than he, and had asked her to marry him. Fearing it was only boyish infatuation, she had refused him, urging that he leave Baltimore and continue his schooling. So here he was.

David helped him find work and a place to live and saw to his enrollment in the University of Chicago. Esther couldn't help but wonder about Morris's reaction to all this; his predictions about the proselytizing female had been fulfilled beyond even his imagination.

They had decided to live off their savings as long as they could so David could give his undivided time to his studies. Ida brought in two dollars a week for room and board, so that helped. And soon Esther began to get acquainted in the neighborhood.

A few houses down the street lived the Schaeffer family, whose children were ragged and hungry half the time because their father gambled his money away. Esther saw the grief and burden Mrs. Schaeffer carried and prayed for an opportunity to reach her. One day as their children played in the fenced-in backyard and the two women drank coffee together, Mrs. Schaeffer herself made the opening.

"I watch your family walk down the street together every Sunday. You are all dressed so nicely. It looks wonderful!"

Esther caught the longing in this lonely woman and felt half guilty in her good fortune.

"When I see you, where are you going?"

Esther prayed for guidance before she answered. She was not sure how their Jewish neighbors might react to their Christian belief. "We are going to church, Mrs. Schaeffer."

"To church? But you are Jewish!"

"Yes, but we are also Christians. We believe that *Yeshua* is the Messiah."

Slowly Joan Schaeffer began to share her problems and disillusionment with Esther. And Esther knew no other response than to tell her to seek help where she had found it: in a living relationship with the Messiah.

One night Esther opened the door to see Joan standing there, her face wet with tears. "Have you seen John?" John was her twelve-year-old son, and she had not seen him since dinner. Now it was ten o'clock, and neither her husband, who was out gambling, or John were home.

Esther went to bring the other Schaeffer children to their apartment, and David and Joan began searching the darkened streets and alleyways.

A few of the neighbors whose sons were friends of John's—and had been asked if they had seen him—joined in the search. But still no one found him. By two o'clock in the morning many of the searchers had returned to the Schaeffers' apartment to suggest that the police be called.

"Joan!" David yelled from the back of the apartment house. "I've found him."

John was sitting at the back door, shivering.

"What are you doing out here? Why didn't you come in?" his mother cried as she put her arms around him.

"I'm waiting for daddy," he answered, his voice hoarse with fatigue and crying. "When daddy comes home, I'll come in."

Slowly his mother and David coaxed him in from the cold landing.

The next day Joan Schaeffer came to see Esther. She could no longer stand to live as she had to without help, and she knew of no one to turn to except the Savior Esther described.

Meanwhile, at Moody, David's experiences were mixed. The school, concentrating on growth and practical experience, was still trying to find its academic moorings. He enjoyed his studies, except for one teacher who made sarcastic cracks about the Jews in his classes. With little knowledge of Judaism and still less understanding, many of the students thought his jokes were uproariously funny. It was not suprising that the fifteen Jewish students quickly sought one another out for support and friendship.

Still another element was entirely strange to these Jewish young people: the discipline. Classes, meals, rising, retiring, study—even leisure—were regulated by the bell. Rules were so numerous, so detailed, that they governed every part of life—their dress, speech, company, and conduct. It was hard enough for the most dedicated

Gentile who was used to Puritan discipline. For the gregarious, indulged Jew, it was impossible. They chafed. They griped. They broke rules. They got into trouble. They made themselves a not-altogether-good reputation at Moody.

One source of irritation was the cafeteria food, which besides being nonkosher was nothing like home. Every day for breakfast they were given oatmeal. Lunch and dinner were little better.

Finally the Jewish students began to protest. When the cafeteria personnel asked, "What would you like?" they'd answer, "A plate." And particularly at breakfast, that's all they took.

What they needed was a good Jewish mother. Who? but Esther. She cooked the familiar *borsht,* the pungent fish cakes, the cereal, and the tender *latkes*—and all were delivered in an atmosphere of the truest *Yiddishkeit.* Sunday after Sunday these students—many of them disowned by their families because of their belief in Christ—converged on the basement apartment. They found a home there, a family. They left their hardlearned English in the red-brick walls of Moody and spoke the familiar, homey Yiddish. And for a while, they were secure on a Jewish island.

Sometimes they paid—ten cents, twenty-five cents—whatever they could. Or someone would bring bagels from the bakery.

With so many to feed, Esther quickly learned to shop on Maxwell Street. Every week she and Ida, baskets on their arms, attacked the market.

They felt at home there. Maxwell Street in 1914 could have been Nikolayev. It was near the train station, and many of the fifty thousand Jews who had come to Chicago in the last twenty years had gone no further. The streets were cluttered with outdoor stalls and tables piled with all kinds of food and clothing. Vendors called their wares above the sounds of horse-drawn wagons rumbling across the bricks with still more fresh country produce and the slow, sharp staccato of the mounted police patrol.

The noise, the dust, the mingled smell of fresh bread, horseradish, sausage, cigars, and wine with the pervasive odor of garlic . . . Esther loved it all. She could haggle with the best. Only the most stupid or an occasional *goy* expected to pay what was asked. The rest were aggressive and on their guard.

"How much is the skirt?"

"For you, two dollars."

"It has a hole in it."

"So, where else can you find a skirt for two dollars?"

Esther and Ida learned who were the truly kosher butchers and what shops carried the freshest chicken. And for $1.50 they walked home with almost more food than they could carry.

So by work and wit, the little family lived . . . closely but well. And the weekly deluge of Moody students only refreshed their own *Yiddishkeit*. Winter came; the furnace heat never seemed to reach their floor. The children were sick. But they dressed warmer and thanked God again that things were no worse.

They learned to move about in the great city. With a few coins and a little *chutzpa* one could get most anywhere on the more than one thousand miles of track for trolley car or elevated train. It was frightening at first, but soon they enjoyed the tall buildings and the museums that told them more in a few hours than they could learn in a year of study. In rare times, and when the weather was warm, they took the children to the lakeshore to watch the boats on the horizon, to feel the cool breeze, and to paddle in the waves.

But if anyone had asked Esther what she thought of Chicago, she would have answered with a shrug, "Some good, some bad," for to admit too much good would have been somehow to threaten it, and that she wasn't about to do.

12 THE GOSPEL WAGON

DURING THOSE YEARS at Moody, even Esther had classes, which wives of Bible students were expected to take, and certain meetings they were expected to attend. Mrs. James M. Gray, the dean's wife, sponsored and supervised these meetings, and Esther soon learned that each member was to take her turn leading a devotional lesson.

"Mrs. Andrews will have the study next week," Mrs. Gray announced, and it didn't take Esther long to realize that *B* was next on the list. She went home in a sweat of apprehension. Though she could talk endlessly in casual conversation, how could she lead a devotional? And in English, yet?

Esther even worried about Mrs. Andrews, who must have also been anxious, for she did not show up for their next session. When Mrs. Gray discovered this, she led the group in Scripture reading, comment, and prayer with graciousness and ease. Esther wondered how anyone could be so rich in knowledge, so calm and sure of herself.

And just as she had expected, "Mrs. Bronstein will have the study next week," Mrs. Gray announced.

Later she moaned to David, "I've never even heard anyone give a devotional before today." Although she had been a Christian for three years, she had never attended a Bible study or anything else at church except Sunday morning service.

"This isn't the way to become a missionary's wife," he reminded her. "I don't know how to do one either, so we'll prepare it together."

During that week they studied and prayed and wrote the devotional together in Yiddish because Esther still couldn't read or write English. It seemed best for Esther to speak about what she knew: the Old Testament prophecies that Jesus fulfilled.

But she deliberately avoided the prophecies of the Messiah's birth that most Christians knew by heart. Instead she began with Psalm 22:14, which predicts the Messiah's death by crucifixion.

I am poured out like water, and all my bones are out of joint: my heart is like wax; it is melted in the midst of my bowels. For dogs have compassed me: the assembly of the wicked have enclosed me: they pierced my hands and my feet. I may tell all my bones; they look and stare upon me.

To some it might seem unusual that a Jew who maintained her Jewishness in everything she did would bring up the crucifixion. But both she and David had lost their guilt once they understood Isaiah 53—that Christ's death fulfilled God's purpose.

As she began to talk about the Scripture she was presenting, Esther held her notes high, the paper shaking slightly in her hands. But the first time she dared look up, she realized that the women seemed to be interested. Suddenly she realized that she had something to give them. Raised a Jew, worshiping as Christ had, she understood and knew some things they didn't. And because Jews still lived in isolated communities, many of these Christian women had never known any Jews or anything about Jewish customs.

Slowly she let the paper drop to her lap; the words came faster now that she spoke without having to translate her Yiddish notes.

She ended the devotional with Psalm 22:27. "All the ends of the world shall remember and turn unto the Lord: and all the kindreds of the nations shall worship before thee."

Here in this room in Chicago, a *shtetl* Jew from Russia—somewhat chubby from bearing two children—told twenty-eight middle-class Christian women what it had been like to find the Messiah. Her presence, the *Yiddishkeit* that surrounded her, testified more than her words to the Lord's promise—"All the ends of the world shall remember and turn unto the Lord."

From then on Esther was asked to speak at different times.

"Mrs. Bronstein," someone would say. "You ought to speak about this. You're Jewish."

For Esther and her people it was a small beginning, but a few Christians began to understand what it meant to be a Jew.

The last term of their two-year stint at Moody brought an experience that would influence their whole life and ministry. It began when they ran out of money. David had to work part-time at the Chicago Hebrew Mission, which had a slight connection with Moody at that time. Moody students often went out with the "gospel wagons" into the surrounding neighborhoods.

Although David worked in the reading room, he knew his turn on the wagon would come. These gospel wagons were horse-drawn platforms, equipped with a pump organ and pulpit. Wherever a crowd would gather, the wagon stopped, and students sang, preached, prayed, and invited sinners to Christ. It was an effective ministry in this teeming, restless city of immigrants.

As a Jew, his gospel wagon duties would center on Jewish neighborhoods. He dreaded his first meeting, so Esther volunteered to go along. As they clattered toward Twelfth Street and Roosevelt Road, he felt his discomfort growing. If these students were as insensitive to the Jewish heart and mind here as they were in the classroom . . . ! And obviously, they regarded him as their star attraction—a kind of "bait." Yet the more experienced students took charge of the service.

David heard the same *goyish* sermons that were delivered to the Irish and Germans and Swedes. The response? What would you expect of Russian Jews who had never heard the name of Jesus except when they were being persecuted? Questions were asked, remarks thrown, and the "evangelists'" answers carried an unmistakable take-it-or-leave-it overtone that could not fail to irritate the hearers.

This was America! The Jews knew they did not have to run; they did not even have to listen. Rumbles of antagonism stirred through the crowd. And David knew his presence made them even more hostile. *Goyim* could be expected to be suckers; but here was this Jew. The rumble grew to boos and jeers.

David and Esther looked at one another. These were their people, and they alone among the Moody students knew they were not unreasonable. But they also knew that mass evangelism would not reach them.

Suddenly someone picked up a rock and threw it. Others joined, throwing overripe vegetables and chunks of pavement—whatever was at hand.

As David turned toward the wagon, he felt a sharp pain between his eyes. Blood clouded his vision, and his head throbbed. One of his companions put his arm around David to steady him, and slowly they walked to a nearby drugstore.

Soon the Jewish druggist began to clean the wound as he scolded David in Yiddish.

"You ought to be ashamed of yourself! You, a good son of Israel, making a fool of yourself with *goyim!*"

David was too stunned and shaken to reply. For the moment, at least, words seemed inappropriate. He winced as the alcohol-soaked cotton cleansed the cut.

"*Meshiach!* What do they know about *Meshiach?* Our fathers have waited for four thousand years, and suddenly they have found him?" The druggist leaned over to study the jagged cut more closely.

"Don't think we need any stitches here," he observed and then continued his harangue.

"And you. Anyone can see you're straight from the *shtetl*. Probably raised in a good synagogue school. Studied the Holy Books. Right?"

David nodded as he felt the gauze and tape pressed into place.

"Take it from me. I'm older than you. Those people, they don't understand us Jews. They'll never push their *Yeshua* off on us!"

David paid the man his fee, and still dazed, limped back onto the wagon with Esther beside him.

As they rode back to the mission headquarters, David thought about how he would reach his people. He knew that some Hebrew-Christian evangelists were great attractions among the Baptist and Methodist audiences in the South. They drew large crowds of the curious, but, admittedly, they made little headway among the Jews.

And he had read a letter in *The Forward,* a Jewish socialist paper from New York—a confession really. The Jewish writer said that he had needed a job when he met a big-bellied, well-dressed Jew who was a Christian missionary to their people.

The missionary told the writer that he could make $175 a month, plus gifts, if he became a missionary.

Without any belief in Jesus Christ and without any knowledge of Christianity, this man had preached to the Jews. David knew that some unscrupulous Jews had paved a treacherous path for the truly converted to follow.

But he also knew that the Jews could be reached. He had been. Only it would take a ministry that met their needs and began with their Jewish beliefs. This was the ministry God had called him to. And slowly God was showing him the way.

"God hit me with a rock," David would testify later, "to teach me not to use street-corner evangelism anymore."

And he never did. He worked for the mission, but never again on the gospel wagon. There had to be a better way. From that time on, his study—the purpose of his mind—was set on finding that way.

After graduation, a job was waiting for David in Baltimore, but his teachers at Moody suggested he go to McCormick Theological Seminary, the nearby Presbyterian school.

This possibility had never occurred to Esther, who had been planning to return to Baltimore. Now David wanted to go to seminary. But their savings were gone. Esther was tired of the everlasting school, the poverty, the long evenings at home. She reasoned. She pleaded. She nagged. But David, having decided, could not be changed.

There was this struggle in him he couldn't explain, even to Esther. Maybe especially to Esther. He was not ready to work among his people. He was still searching, studying, praying for the secret that would open the Jewish heart to Jesus. He knew, too, that to be accepted and respected by the Jewish community he must have unquestioned academic qualifications. Their rabbis were men steeped in holy literature; they would expect no less of someone who wanted them to listen to another way.

Like most women, Esther longed for security. She suspected that Christ expected her to overcome this longing. But the pain of the *shtetl* was still too vivid. She had waited patiently for David to provide this security, but somehow he never had.

So she had reached out to her Savior in prayer asking for his love and care. And she had felt his presence and guidance when no one else had been able to help her.

Now she reminded herself of the assurance of his help. And it was as if he whispered to her, "Don't worry. Trust in me!"

He seemed to suggest something else, too. "Moses was eighty years old before he began his ministry, and he led his people out of Egypt to the Promised Land. Have patience, *mein kind.*"

So Esther settled down to see David through. She sewed. She trimmed hats. She tretched every nickel ten ways. The Presbyterian seminary promised him $100 a term. Fourth Presbyterian Church, the church they had attended during their years at Moody, subsidized them with another hundred. Ida still lived with them and added her board payment, and David continued to work for Chicago Hebrew Mission.

They got along. They made do. And in the process of resolving their differences and difficulties, their mutual love and respect found its level: they worked out a solid relationship, a practical, mutually supportive combination that would sustain a lifetime of ministry.

The three years passed quickly. Esther took courses appropriate to ministers' wives. She learned to preside at meetings. Both of the children were in school now, and she had time to take in more sewing.

Meanwhile, Jacob finished at the University of Chicago and enrolled two years behind David at the seminary. He had convinced Ruby Gaither that his love was more than an infatuation, and they had been married after his graduation.

By then, newspapers were blaring world-war headlines, and twenty thousand Jewish men from Chicago served their adopted country in the armed forces. The Russian Revolution, with implications they did not dare imagine, blazed a fiery trail. Isaac Peltz, Esther's half brother, arrived in New York with one daughter; the rest of his family had been executed by the Russian revolutionists. And Israel Peltz, at the age of seventy-eight, had remarried and was living near New York.

In the spring of 1919 David was ordained at the Fourth Presbyterian Church, a Gothic, cathedral-like structure on posh Michigan Avenue. Esther sat in a pew near the front, wondering at the path their life together had taken. Here was her husband, David, in long black robes, the hint of a smile tugging at his mouth, standing straight beside the solemn-faced leaders of the Presbytery.

He had studied hard for the ordination exam and had

appeared before a committee to be questioned. Now he stood behind the long oak table in the chancel and publicly answered the questions.

"Do you trust in Jesus Christ your Savior, acknowledge him head of the world, the head of the church . . ." and on the minister intoned.

"I do." David stole a glance at Esther as he answered.

"Will you seek to serve the people?" His mind wandered. The path was not altogether clear, but he was ready. He had his own ideas on how to reach his people, beyond what he had learned at Bible school and seminary.

Finally the moderator pronounced the long awaited words. Looking straight into David's clear eyes he told him, "Now you are a minister of the word in the church. Whatever you do, in word or deed, do everything in the name of the Lord Jesus, giving thanks to God the Father through him. Amen."

It was over, and Esther walked the long aisle and out into the bright spring light of Michigan Avenue, her heart swelling with pride.

17 NEWARK

THE PROBLEM NOW BECAME: Where could David best work with his revolutionary ideas for reaching his people? He knew he could not work within an organization that dictated procedure or placed restraints on his experimental methods. Although he received calls from other denominations, David stayed with the Presbyterian church. There, he sensed, he would be given the most freedom.

And of the choices he had, David felt God wanted them in Newark, New Jersey, where a Jewish mission had struggled for several years without success. The Reverend E. S. Greenbaum was working there, and David knew that they shared similar ideas and would function well as a team.

But after five years, Esther felt comfortable in Chicago. Hannah, now seven, and Morris, ten, were happy with their school and friends. Her brother Jacob was a junior in seminary, and Ida was a student at Moody Bible Institute. Chicago was her home—even more than Baltimore had been.

Again she was frustrated. But not as much as before. At least David was beginning his ministry.

So after some struggling and some attempt to persuade David that God might be calling them to stay in Chicago, Esther adapted to the inevitable. After all, her father and his third wife and family lived in nearby New York, and maybe he would accept her now.

So, cumbersome and uncomfortable with her third pregnancy, she struggled through the summer heat, packing the few possessions they could afford to move and selling those that were not worth moving. When the time came to leave, she had $200 in cash plus $200 loaned them by the Fourth Presbyterian Church.

As their taxi from the Newark depot approached their new field of work, her heart sank.

"Oh, no, David! A Jewish work—here?"

Maybe the neighborhood had been Jewish when the mission was started, but it was not now. "The children are black, not Jewish!"

Their calling, their preparation was for work among their people; they were convinced that only Jews could reach Jews, and it would follow that a black population also needed someone of their own race.

"We can't work here!" She wavered between disappointment and anger.

David covered his own shock. Surely the mission board would know better than to pour effort and money into a Jewish ministry where there were no Jews. He had heard, too, that some previous workers—obviously not understanding the Jew or, to David's mind, misled in their methods—had used the standard evangelistic routine that had caused him so much grief in Chicago. Could this bad image be overcome?

"And the buildings!" Esther, overtired, could see only the worst. "They look as if nobody cared for them. And they're so churchy!"

No wonder the Jews of the neighborhood—such few as remained—looked on the mission with indifference or disdain. But they were here now, she and David and the children, because they—at least David—believed God had led them to Newark. She would make the best of it.

Their $400 didn't allow for a luxurious beginning. They took over one of the clubhouses on the church property, making do with two upstairs bedrooms and a kitchen and living room downstairs. They bought beds, a table and chairs, and a comfortable rocking chair for Esther.

Never mind that the heat was stifling—even more humid than in Chicago—and that mosquitoes swarmed through their unscreened windows. They soon considered themselves settled, and while David and Reverend Greenbaum devised their working plans, Esther looked about to see what she could do.

She began by mingling with the children who came to the playground, and then she started sewing classes for the girls. Next came vacation Bible school; she helped David and Reverend Greenbaum with the classes, until the baby arrived—another boy whom they named David, Jr.

Still her work did not slacken. She kept the baby beside

her or posted Morris to watch him.

And as Esther had hoped, she did see more of her family. Once they found an apartment, she called her father's home. Israel still would not talk to her. But as she continued to call, Esther became friendly with his new wife, "Bubba."

Finally Bubba, curious about this rebel daughter whom Israel refused to discuss, agreed to visit Esther. Their first visit was strained. Esther knew nothing about her new stepmother, and Bubba wanted to learn everything she could about Esther.

But soon Bubba and her daughters visited as frequently as Esther's family had in Baltimore. Evenings, after the younger children were in bed, David found their guests to be interested listeners as he explained the Christ of the New Testament.

It was their fifth Saturday together when Bubba said, "Next week we'll come on Friday, if that's all right with you. I want Israel to hear this, too, and he won't travel on the Sabbath."

Esther was amazed at Bubba's announcement; she had never told them that Israel discussed their visits with her. But he did, and Bubba was sure that with a little more persuasion, he would come.

Esther could only wonder at God's providence. Their move to Newark, where she didn't want to be, had brought this opportunity to see her father for the first time in seven years. It was too wonderful. She pushed her usual Friday baking ahead to Thursday so she could serve *challeh* to her guests.

Later Bubba described Israel Peltz's excuses, his arguments, and his refusal to speak after they began their trip to Esther's. But once the door opened and he saw his daughter—wearing glasses he had no idea she needed, her hair bobbed short, and two of her children at her side—he held her in his arms.

"Your mama should see you now," he muttered between joyful sobs.

If papa had looked old to Esther in the Baltimore train station so long ago, he should have then. But instead of seeing the new stoop to his shoulders or the thinning white hair, Esther saw the appreciative look in his eyes and heard the low resonant tone of his voice. Her father had always loved his self-sufficient, aggressive daughter. Now she knew that nothing had changed.

So week after week Esther had the joy of watching her father and his family hear David explain the Word of God in the New Testament.

One week, after they had left, she asked David, "What do you think? Is my father beginning to believe?"

"I'm not sure, Esther. Sometimes I think so; then again he is so attached to *shul* that even if he believed in his heart, I don't think he could break away. It's harder for the older people."

Esther could understand that. And when Bubba and her daughters became open believers and were baptized, and still Israel held back, she did not despair.

Sometimes now she saw Joey, who would come to New York and stay with both families. These visits excited Esther, who felt both a great love for her youngest brother and a sense of guilt at having failed him when he had needed her. Maybe, now, God would give her another chance.

In her same aggressive manner, Esther kept after Joey at each visit.

"Look, Uncle David is a Christian, and he's still a Jew. You can be both, too."

One day Joey approached her with a plan for his future.

"I'll graduate from high school in a few months,

111

Esther," he began, "and you know what I want to do? I want to go to school in New York and learn to be a lawyer."

Joey a lawyer? Next to being a doctor, it was the greatest future her Yiddish heart could imagine. And this time she could help.

"You can, Joey, you can!" she told him. But for him to do so, she had to persuade Reverend Greenbaum and David that Joey should work at the mission as a youth worker so he would have a source of income.

"He doesn't have to be a Christian now," Esther argued with David when they discussed the possibility. "He's beginning to believe, and there are several boys working at the mission who aren't. Anyway, he's been working at the orphanage as a youth counselor."

Finally David and Reverend Greenbaum agreed.

But no one had counted on Joey's exuberance. With more enthusiasm than wisdom he told of his plans in his graduation speech and implied that he was beginning to believe that Jesus was the Messiah.

Soon Joey was back in New York, but not to stay. "I can't come, Esther. They won't let me, and I'm not of age. Until I'm eighteen, I'm still in the home's custody."

Nothing Esther could say would change the superintendent's mind. The boldness and persistence that had often been effective only hardened the authorities more. So Joey continued to work for the orphanage as a counselor, but every weekend he came to visit Esther and David.

Then the home notified her that a social worker would visit them to determine if Joey could even continue to see them.

Esther welcomed the brisk Jewish woman with a feeling of futility. *I can't be something I'm not,* she thought. *I will have to answer her questions honestly.*

Notebook in hand, the woman uttered a brief greeting and then began to walk about the mission, examining the meeting rooms, the playground, and the assembly hall.

"I don't see any crucifix or images," she said, plainly puzzled. "Are you sure you're Christian?"

"We're not that kind of Christian," Esther explained. "We are still Jews. We keep a kosher home and believe just as all Jews, except we know that Jesus is the Messiah."

The social worker went with Esther to their apartment. And after a tour of their small quarters—during which Esther saw her notice the Torah and other Holy Books on their bookshelves—Esther invited her to have some bagels and lox.

Esther never knew what the woman reported to the orphanage; but Joey was told that he could continue to visit them, although he must remain in the home until he was of age.

Meanwhile the mission in Newark struggled on. But progress was slow. They were reaching people—helping those around them—but not in the way they had expected. In the two years they were in Newark, few accepted Christ as Savior. And the majority of people they came in contact with were not Jewish. Still David was honing his understanding of the Bible—particularly the Old Testament prophecies and their fulfillments in Jesus Christ.

One day Dr. Stuart Conning, head of the Presbyterian Jewish work, called David and Esther into the Board of National Missions office.

"Would you be willing to move back to Chicago and head the work in the Jewish community there?" he began. "We have a church there—the old Eleventh Presbyterian," he continued. "The Gentile Christians have moved to the suburbs, and now it is in a Jewish area. . . . Would you like to go to Chicago, and look it over?"

David agreed as they both tried to hide their relief until David knew what the work would involve.

"You know how much I'd like to go back," Esther told David later. "There are lots of Jews there," she reminded him, as if he needed reminding. "And Newark has never really been our home."

What she said was true. Five years in Chicago had moved their hearts toward that city and the tens of thousands of Jews on Chicago's North Side.

Chicago! It was good to walk the familiar streets again; David had that comfortable feeling of being at home. Catching a streetcar to the Humboldt Park area, he got off close to the old Eleventh Presbyterian Church at 1241 Washtenaw. *This is my place!* he said to himself, seeing the long rows of Jewish shops on Division Street, hearing the familiar Yiddish all around him. Small wonder the Presbyterians had decided to make the old church a Jewish mission.

"More than fifty thousand Jews live in the immediate vicinity," Dr. Conning had told him.

And there was the church. "Immanuel Hall," a sign in the yard announced. But it was old, dilapidated, and dirty, and the structure was unmistakably Christian: the red brick building was outlined in white, with arched windows and a steeple. Inside, an auditorium with a platform at one end was furnished with typical church pews, a communion table, and a pulpit.

Several Sunday school rooms clustered in the rear. But a large vacant lot on one side excited David. Already his mind was seeing a community center, which he was sure would reach this great Jewish population.

But was the community already disillusioned, as in Newark? David didn't think so. Little had been done in the few years the church had been a Jewish mission.

David met the caretaker, a man who lived in the back rooms and watched over the property. He walked about the neighborhood, listening to the children at play, watching the women come and go to market, noting the strong Orthodox element in the dress and demeanor of the residents.

Marriage brokers' offices peered from between kosher butcher shops and Yiddish bookstores. Synagogues, from the most pretentious to those that were little more than storefronts, appeared with the regularity of a giant's footsteps. Yes, this was a ready field!

All the way back to Newark David's mind invented possibilities for the old church. He sketched on dining car napkins. He figured in his pocket notebook. But he must not let himself be carried away. Was Chicago really God's plan for them?

The next day he talked with Dr. Conning, who explained the church's short history as a mission.

"After the Christians left, we hired a man to raise money for the work among the Jews. After two years, all he had was 1700 names on a list and no money."

"You are offering me a headache," David said, knowing that although the work appealed to him, nothing had been done. "Do you have a budget for me, or are you going to leave me out in the cold?"

"David," Conning replied, "I love you like a son. You've got something God is going to use. I can give you $1,500 for a budget, but I can't promise anything else. We'll try to get the Presbytery of Chicago to help us if everything works out."

When David returned home, he found the confirmation he needed in Esther's eyes. "I think God wants us to take the Chicago work, sweetheart," he said, voicing both their thoughts.

ESTHER

It was the news she wanted to hear. True, her loyalties were torn. Her father and his wife were in New York, and Joey was nearby. But her heart had never left Chicago. She could close her eyes and see the familiar streets, hear the screech of the trolley, and smell the acrid soft-coal smoke. There they would be among their people. There they could begin to practice what long years of study and experience had taught them.

"I'll start packing," she replied.

14 IMMANUEL HALL

BUT CHICAGO HELD a few unpleasant surprises. First, the Bronsteins discovered that $1,200 of the $1,500 Dr. Conning had promised had already been spent on the caretaker's wages. Only $300 was left.

"Lord, tell us what to do," they prayed as they visited the neighborhood each day of the next week. Slowly they became convinced that the people would never come to the church on their own. Besides, the entire building needed to be cleaned and painted.

So they decided to direct their efforts toward the children, who had no place to play. The $300 was used to fence in the large vacant lot next to the church and buy two swings, a teeter-totter, and a sandbox. As they began erecting the fence and assembling the swings, the neighborhood children began to stop by—first just gazing from across the street, then sitting on the curb asking an occasional question, and finally "helping" with the construction. By July 14 the playground was ready.

Soon children who had been scattered on the streets, dodging traffic or kicking cans along cluttered sidewalks, converged on the area.

Oh, no! Not so early! was Esther's first reaction. For before she had her family fed and dressed, sounds drifted to their rooms at the rear of the church from the playground—sounds that demanded her attention.

Never an early riser, the ordeal of supervising these crowding, shouting, sometimes quarreling, children so early in the morning often seemed more than she could endure. And as the day progressed, so did the temperature. The playground was mercilessly exposed to the sun and the accumulated heat of the nearby brick buildings.

"What would we do without Morris?" Esther commented to David, who had left his study one particularly hot, humid morning to help.

Morris, now twelve and nearly as tall as his father, was coaching a ball game in one corner of the lot. Hannah was playing with some girls her age and watching little David, who toddled everywhere he shouldn't. And David and Esther manned the swings as the children lined up to be pushed. Twenty pushes each. And with each push, Esther and David prayed for that particular child.

Sometimes the lines seemed endless. Esther's arms ached, and the heat from the sun beat unceasingly. If only they could take the children into the church! But they dared not. These were Jewish children. And despite the acceptance of the playground, a church was a church. They could not risk alienating the neighbors by taking their children into the building.

Finally one torrid day, one of the mothers who had come to watch suggested, "Why don't you take the children inside? It's much cooler in there," she commented.

"Do you think it would be all right? It sure is hot out here," Esther replied.

"Go ahead! Anyone can see you're not going to hurt them."

"David!" Esther called when the woman had gone. "Our prayers have been answered. Mrs. Cohen said we should take the kids in the church, where it's cooler."

Still David hesitated.

"Well, *I'm* going in!" She was miserable and had a headache from the sun. A few of the bolder children followed, then some others, and soon, from the corner of her eye, Esther saw David enter, wipe the sweat from his face, and settle down as she had to a quieter game.

The same children were back the next day, so nobody could have cared too much. After that they often took the children inside, where they would tell stories or work at craft projects.

"So many children, David! We should have a vacation Bible school like we did in Newark," Esther suggested a few days later.

"I don't think we should call it that, and I wonder if the parents would let their children come."

"It won't hurt to try. We'll call it summer school—maybe that will help."

So they put up a sign advertising "Vacation Summer School." Maybe the neighbors saw this as free child care. More likely the children themselves, many of them left to roam the streets while their parents worked, took the initiative.

Whatever the reason, the next Friday Esther finished a long day of writing registration cards and sat at the kitchen table counting and sorting them. The cards stuck to her sweaty fingers. Her dress felt rumpled and soggy.

"David." Her voice dropped with weariness when she ought to be happy. "David. We have 220 children coming next week. What will we do with them?"

Success. Was it worth the price? David, Jr., was crying, his supper overdue. From the next room she could hear Hannah and Morris quarreling. The lunch dishes still sat in the sink, and she ached in every muscle.

"What will we do, David?"

"I'll talk to Dr. Brown tomorrow. Surely someone will help." Dr. Henry Seymour Brown was head of the church extension board in Chicago, and any requests for help went through him.

He promised seventy-five dollars toward the pay for each teacher they could recruit for the five-week session and even suggested one young woman. "She's not a teacher, but she can help."

So the night before school was to begin, the three of them and Morris, who was called in as an assistant, pooled their inexperience.

"We'll learn together," David said, and they prayed for the strength and wisdom they surely needed.

The classes were held in the auditorium. The children sat stiff-legged on the pews or squirmed or stood or crawled about. When one of them began to laugh, the others joined in.

Finally Esther grabbed one of the worst offenders by the arm.

"Do you act like this at home?" she demanded.

"No," the young tousle-haired boy admitted. "But this is a missionary place, so it's all right."

So the children and their parents were only taking advantage of them, using them—all the while laughing at their willingness to be used. Depression ached through her as she thought of her own neglected children.

And they had four weeks to go!

But soon they met a professional teacher who knew how to encourage better behavior and took the lead in organizing the sessions.

David would begin the day with lessons on the Old Testament, reaching the children, as he would someday reach their parents, through prophecy. Then they divided into several activities: woodwork, sewing, and even hammock making. The Jewish parents, hearing their children recite portions of their own Scripture, were not alarmed by the sessions.

The final assembly was something Esther would always remember. David was testing the children.

"What do the Bible stories tell about?"

"A king!" the children shouted.

"And who was the king?"

"Jesus!" they replied.

One day soon after vacation school was over, a little girl named Pearl shyly approached Esther. "Can you come and visit my mother?"

Such a simple request. But Esther was terrified. What if Mrs. Applebaum didn't want to see her? She could be thrown out, insulted.

For a few days she thought about it. And she was as much afraid of saying something that might deserve rejection as she was of being repulsed because she was a Christian.

One evening she sought the answer in Scripture, paging through the Bible until she came to Psalm 32, which seemed to be speaking to her.

I will instruct you and teach you the way you should go;

ESTHER

I will counsel you with my eye upon you.
Be not like a horse or a mule, without understanding,
which must be curbed with bit and bridle,
else it will not keep with you.

Who had the stubborn, aggressive nature described in that passage but her? The words she was reading would remain in her mind forever. For curbing her own nature, following the Lord's way—which was often stiller and more quiet—was a task to be done each day of her life. Her nature never seemed to change, but only the hand that governed it. When she failed, it was because she had forgotten, not that she didn't care.

So because she knew it was His will, she went. She slowly climbed the stairs to the third-floor apartment, fearing what might happen in the next minutes.

Her first knock seemed unheard. Maybe they weren't home.

But she had best try again. This time a voice called, "Who's there?"

"Pearlie's teacher," she replied.

The door opened just a crack—plainly not an invitation to enter. But through the crack Esther could see a darling black-haired baby.

"What a beautiful baby!" she cried. "You should enter him in the *Tribune* baby contest!"

"Do you really think so?" and the door was open to a visit she and Mrs. Applebaum both enjoyed. Never after that was Esther afraid. She knew the Holy Spirit would show her how to reach those she called on, and in the next months, she and David made hundreds of calls.

Soon neighbors began to stop in at the back door that led to their apartment—not nearly so threatening as the church's front door. And once they were inside, they smelled the kosher food she was cooking or the *challeh* that was cooling on the counter. She would chat with them in Yiddish as they enjoyed a piece of her bread. Their home was as Jewish as any in the block, and people felt right about being there.

For Esther and David had not abandoned their *Yiddishkeit* when they became Christians. Esther, like David, saw her new faith as an extension of the old.

Holding onto the old Jewish ways by keeping a kosher home and cherishing the Old Testament Scripture kept them a part of the long continuum that had begun with Abraham. After all, she had found Jesus to be the *Meshiach:* the final revelation of God she had been waiting for. She hadn't become a Christian to escape her Jewishness—as some *shtetl* Jews had Americanized—but to complete it.

That first summer also saw the beginnings of what would be one of their greatest ministries: the camp in Saugatuck, Michigan, about 160 miles from Chicago on Lake Michigan's eastern shore. What better place for children who lived in a crowded world of concrete than Camp Gray's 140 acres of natural woodland and sand dunes?

"What if the neighbors won't let their children go?" Esther kept asking David as they began to plan for their first two-week session. But soon twelve girls had signed up, and they had their parents' permission.

There were endless plans to make. Instead of the three or four that could have been taken in a car, they now had twelve, plus their own family. A bus was rented. Food was bought, and plans were made so each day would be filled: hikes to Mount "Baldy"—Old Mount Baldhead, Michigan's highest sand mountain—and the "haunted house," campfires, stunt nights, and time to study the Scriptures with David and alone.

The girls came by the mission every day—so excited

they were—and the envy of the neighborhood. Not often did these children get a chance to climb sand dunes and find their way through tangled Indian trails.

And once they got to Camp Gray, they were not disappointed. There were long walks—each girl waiting her turn to hold Mrs. B's hand. Intimate talks. Long evenings of learning to know one another.

Too soon, it was time to return. The bus arrived, loaded the reluctant campers, and started on the five-hour journey home. After the first hour the girls were quiet. Esther, her head resting on David's shoulder, squeezed his hand to get his attention.

"Sweetheart," she whispered, "it was a wonderful camp!"

"Yes, but aren't you very tired? I don't know how you kept up with the girls' demands."

"Sure I'm tired, but happy, too. Don't you see? . . . This is something we can do every year. The girls will tell their parents and friends. There are so many. . . ." Her voice trailed off into unspoken dreams.

David could not help smiling. As so often before, she had spoken what he was thinking. What an opportunity! They could have groups—boys, girls, even adults. In such a setting, away from the church, they could talk about the things of God intimately. Surely God had used this experimental camp to show them his direction.

And while David thought of his teaching and ministry, Esther dreamed of new buildings that they could use whenever they wanted. A whole compound just for their mission right here in Michigan. Dining room, dormitories, cottages, a chapel—maybe even a little home of their own. It would happen. God would help them make it happen.

When David spoke, it was like a continuation of her own thoughts. "We'll call it *Peniel*, 'the face of God.' "

THE FORUM

AT FIRST THE ADULTS in the community ignored the activity at Immanuel Hall, which David quickly renamed Goodwill Community Center. But slowly Sunday gatherings that began with just the family included a few neighbors, particularly the children. And as the interest increased, resistance began.

A butcher shop was located across the street from the church, and soon the butcher's wife began standing out front on Sunday, tormenting those who approached the church.

"Don't go in there," she yelled at some of the children one day. "They'll put a curse on you." Then she spat at them.

Esther tried to dissuade the butcher's wife; then she appealed to David. "Do something for her so she'll not be against us."

One day just before a Jewish holiday, the older woman was standing on the street corner holding more bundles of meat than she seemed able to carry.

David stopped the old car they had recently purchased and asked where she was going.

"I'm waiting for a streetcar," she answered. "I have to deliver these bundles to Logan Square for the holiday."

"Get in," David replied. "I'll take you."

"What? To Logan Square? But that's so far!" she protested as she came toward the car door.

"This is my car, and it goes where I tell it to go," David said pleasantly.

He drove her to Logan Square and, for the next few hours, took her to the various homes to deliver her orders.

Two days later as the Jewish community gathered to celebrate the Day of Atonement, members of the synagogue began talking about the Bronsteins.

"They're stealing the souls of our children," one mother warned the group.

Slowly the butcher stood. "Look here," he said. "That man is more than a rabbi to me. . . . Did a rabbi ever take my wife to deliver meat? No. But Mr. Bronstein helped her deliver some of the meat you ordered for the holiday. Can you find a better Jew than that?"

With this bit of acceptance, David began going to the park on California Avenue, just a block away. Esther did not understand exactly what went on there except that someone would stand on a box and talk, and sometimes the men got very excited or even fought. One evening, just as she was putting the last stitches in a dress for Hannah, she heard David's step on the pavement. She knew by his brisk pace that he had something to tell her.

"Esther! You should have been there!"

Now why should she go to a place like that? Who wanted to talk about politics?

"I spoke, Esther, and they listened to me!"

"You didn't preach!"

"Of course not. Nobody would stay, or I'd get pelted with tomatoes if I tried. I talked about what they talked about, and some of them asked me questions about our work here."

"Then you preached?"

"They'd never take that. I only answered their questions; but they were interested!"

Of course! Who wouldn't be interested in David, who knew more than a whole park full of men? A real *chacham*, her David!

"Esther, I've been thinking. Why don't we do something like that here? Have a discussion. A forum. I think they will come—especially when the weather gets colder."

Only a few weeks later, with the pews and every reminder of its former function as a church gone from the inside, David nailed a large poster to the door: "Socialism: What Is It and Where Does It Come From?"

Most people in their area were Eastern European Jews, many of them from Russia. Ever since the Bolshevik Revolution in 1917, these Jews had been questioning the strange political philosophies coming out of Europe. Many remembered the socialism that had begun to permeate Russia before they had immigrated. It had sounded good: all that talk of the common good. But it had spawned the revolution and the Communist movement that had killed many of their relatives still in Russia. No one knew quite what to think.

"People want to talk about socialism these days, so

that's what we'll talk about," David said as he explained his choice to Esther. "If we can even get them inside the building, we've gone a long way."

The two of them prayed as they went about putting the last chair in place and checking again to make sure that not a single motto, poster, altar object, or book was in sight that could set anyone against being there.

Esther dressed with even more than usual care, patting the curl in her brown hair, smoothing her very best dress. Would anyone come? And if they didn't, what would she and David do next?

Slowly at first, two men, then a few more—mostly from the California Avenue debates—drifted into the assembly hall.

As the time to begin came closer, men and a few women began coming in fours and fives. The next time Esther looked up from greeting people at the door, the room was filled with working men and the few women.

David walked over to the piano and picked up the Bible that lay on top. Then he went to the pulpit and raised the Bible above his head.

"Are any of you Christians?" he began.

Esther was amazed at his blunt approach.

When the only response was silence, David asked another question. "Can any of you measure up as socialists?"

Several responded "Yes" before David went on.

"This," and he waved the Bible in the air, "this is the place where you will find real socialism. . . . But don't sneer at it because it's different than the socialism we see today."

Esther saw David look around the hall, and she knew he was measuring their reaction. Could he continue? Would they accept more, or would their rejection be so great he would destroy their modest beginning?

But besides being rather stunned at his approach, many faces seemed to be concentrating on what he was saying, waiting for his next words.

"The men that surrounded Jesus of Nazareth were of all kinds—fishermen, the hated tax collectors, and the revolutionaries of Judaism, the Zealots. But these differences were molded into a group of unified followers who sold everything they had and held it in common."

For a few minutes, he amplified his statements with illustrations from the New Testament. *What a miracle,* Esther thought. *These people are here, and they are listening.*

Then David looked at the group before him. "I'd like to hear from one socialist. . . . What I'd like to know is, is this the socialism you are practicing today?" And he turned the pulpit over to the others who came forward—Blind Levin, an atheist who blended Shakespearean quotations with the sharpest puns, and Louis Aronson, a well-educated infidel who prefaced his remarks with "Mr. Bronstein, I like you. That's why I'd like to speak. To set you and the others straight." Then he assured David, "I won't talk too long," although he did.

That first day Esther was not able to follow many of the arguments. She knew little of socialistic theory. But she began to feel as if the Lord wanted her to say something, to add her testimony to David's, even though the other women who were present kept quiet.

She approached the pulpit and then stood at the side, letting other speakers go before her until no one else came. Then she began to speak in Yiddish—as they all had—softly at first but gathering momentum as the thoughts came.

"You know I'm Jewish. I keep kosher. And when I was twelve, I believed the socialistic talk that was beginning to spread through Russia. My brothers spoke about it frequently in our home. To those of us who were *shtetl* Jews, socialism seemed to speak of freedom."

She looked up to make sure she had their attention, for what she would say next was the only reason she had risen to speak.

"Now I know that socialism is not the answer. If people would believe in the Messiah Jesus Christ, our world would be at peace for we would love one another."

She felt David's approving look as she stepped down, and others rose to speak.

Soon David suggested that they resume their discussions another day, and many began to leave. On the way out, one woman that Esther recognized as a neighbor separated from the crowd and moved toward Esther. She noted that the woman was small and dark with a profile that had an edge like a saw. Her hair, pulled severely back, exaggerated her sharpness. As soon as she reached Esther, the woman's mouth twisted into an ironic frown.

"Do you believe in Jesus Christ?" The question was a demand.

"Yes," Esther replied. And though she was afraid, she felt her eyes brighten with the intensity of her faith.

Without another word, without giving Esther any opportunity to explain, the woman spat in Esther's face. Then she turned and left with the others.

Esther sensed that people were looking at her over their shoulders as she mopped the spittle from her face. The indignity of someone's saliva hot on her cheeks was worse than a slap or physical assault. Esther tried to be calm, but she trembled and fought back the tears. It was not her nature to be submissive, to turn the other cheek. As a youngster in the *shtetl,* she had often won in a good fight, and frequently her verbal retort had silenced her oppressors. But she knew she must not yell out or respond in any way. *God, help me!* she cried deep inside her. *They spit on Jesus, too,* came the answer.

Somehow she managed to face the next person who spoke to her—this one kindly and with a hint of apology.

Days passed before she could remember that moment without shuddering. And by then David had posted another sign announcing the next meeting. Could she bear to go? Could she risk what might be a worse insult?

Daily she held onto the words, "Thou art my hiding place, thou shalt preserve me from trouble; thou shalt compass me about with songs of deliverence."

And each day she knew her Lord was the only hiding place she had. She could not run.

Soon after the forum began, Esther knew the woman was there. She felt her presence, even before she saw her. And after the meeting, the woman approached her. *Oh, Lord,* Esther thought, *I don't know if I can take it again.* The tension within her rose to an unbearable pressure in each of her temples.

"Why didn't you spit back at me?" the woman began, her voice louder than those around them. Again the question was a demand.

But at least this time she let Esther respond. Esther looked into the hard, threatening dark eyes. "My answer is in the New Testament, in Jesus' teachings. . . ."

Esther could go no further without some response from the blunt face before her. She feared this woman's reaction as she had feared few others. For within her Esther sensed all the hatred she had once felt.

Maybe that was why she had been able to control her temper. Esther knew how her words had threatened this woman's being, for Esther herself had hated her husband and Ruby Gaither with that same passion. And she had been rejected in much the same manner by members of her own family. Yet she still loved them, and somehow she would love this woman, too.

But the woman only stood there, her head lowered. At

last she spoke in a voice that was almost plaintive. "Could you loan me one of your books?"

"If you'll wait a minute, I'll get one from our rooms," Esther replied. Then she moved quickly toward the back of the church and David's bookshelves, her head clearing as she realized what had occurred.

"Here," she said as she returned with a Yiddish New Testament.

The woman accepted the book with eagerness and yet reluctance. Esther, noticing that she turned her back so the others could not see, lowered her voice.

"If you have any questions or want to talk about it, come over anytime." She watched her neighbor mingle with the crowd, the book hidden under her coat.

The forums grew beyond expectation. David brought in speakers from the seminary—teachers and ministers—who spoke on subjects of the day. Then the platform was open to any and all.

They never knew what would happen. No matter how revolutionary a speaker's politics might be, no matter how anti-Christian his theology, each was given the right to speak. Arguments erupted. Sometimes fists swung. And other times the meetings ended outside in the street, with the police close at hand. But more and more the discussion would veer toward Christianity, and nearly always one or two would stay afterward to talk with David about his strange belief that made him a Christian but not a goy.

Representatives from the Presbytery came, and David time and again was challenged.

"This is no church! You were called to serve a Christian church!"

David explained patiently. "Give me time to build a church. Meanwhile the people are talking to me, and they hear me."

"But what do you talk about? Socialism? Politics? Education? Labor?"

"I listen to them; they listen to me. They respect what I have to say because I respect their opinion. Look. I can't come insulting them. They would shut me out. Give me time!"

His request was not a plea. Not David. He knew he was right. Hadn't God himself taught him how to reach his people?

"What can you lose?" David reminded them. "The mission was doing nothing before."

Outmaneuvered, but not approving, the church officials retreated to build another offense.

But even those ministers who came to speak were often condescending, although that changed as they saw results. David worked out a strategy. His speakers' "pay" for the evening was an advance meal in a Jewish restaurant. For David saw his call as twofold: telling the Jews about Jesus, and teaching Christians about the Jews and their customs. So David purposely took these Christian speakers to kosher restaurants where little but Jewish food was offered.

One minister ordered *kishkee,* which he thought so good that he kept asking what it was.

David avoided the question several times gracefully but was finally forced to answer.

"Cow's intestines," he replied.

The minister could not overcome his repulsion.

But most of the speakers enjoyed this opportunity to learn about a culture they had too long ignored. And David used the Yiddish surroundings to explain the background and interests of those who would be attending that evening's forum. For David realized that if Gentiles were to communicate their faith to Jews, they must first understand them.

THE FACE OF GOD

THE WOMAN WHO HAD spat on Esther remained constantly in her mind and prayers. How could she reach her and others like her without inspiring hatred? She knew that many of the women were lonely, often cut off from family and friends who were still in Europe. Again the answer seemed to be a social function.

But it would have to be supported by some of the local Jewish women, so Esther went to Pearlie's mother for help.

"Mrs. Applebaum, we'd like to have a party on Saturday for some of the women. Would you come and bring a few friends?"

The first "mothers' party" was small, but the reaction

was enthusiastic, and soon it became a monthly event that was a major social gathering in the neighborhood.

Now Esther needed help. And she saw this need as a way to involve Gentile Christians with Jews. She approached one of the Presbyterian pastors in the city.

"Look," she said in her somewhat abrasive but usually persuasive manner. "We have more than we can do. Your people say they love the Jews? Let me tell your Ladies Aid Society how they can help us."

But once she had secured the pastor's permission, she was overcome by the thought of speaking to the group. She could picture the setting without even being there. A room full of literate, well-dressed *goyim*. And she was a rather plump, dowdy Jewish Christian who usually spoke to groups in Yiddish. She—an immigrant who had never completed high school—would persuade them?

The more she thought about it the more afraid she became. Her naturally positive attitude about herself— many would say overconfidence—often led her into situations that it might have been wise to avoid.

When the day came, she stood before the group she had pictured, and her delivery was not any better than she had imagined. English was not her native tongue, and she did not speak it frequently enough for her speech to be fluent. The notes she held were written in Yiddish just as they had been that day at Mrs. Stone's many years ago. Slowly she translated them as she spoke, beginning to describe the Washtenaw Avenue neighborhood and their work there.

She ended by describing the progress they had made.

"The Jewish mothers are coming to my parties— dozens of them—maybe soon a hundred. But I can't take care of them alone—entertain them, feed them lunch, and tell them about the Lord all at one time. . . . I need your help."

It wasn't her rhetoric or her polish that convinced them, but the force of her love and her desire to reach her people. Eventually, twelve Presbyterian churches were taking their turn in providing food and sending volunteers to serve, baby-sit, and lead the games.

Yes, games. Esther's strategy was to begin with strenuous play in which the women got to know one another and her—and incidentally became so tired they were ready to sit and listen.

Then came her turn. *I can't talk like David,* she reasoned, but she could tell a simple Bible story or what faith in Christ had meant to her and her home.

Later when she had to go to Presbyterian Hospital for surgery, she found a way to extend her ministry to these women.

"I'm responsible for a group of women who don't speak English," she told the doctor there. "I would like to bring them to see you when they need medical help."

The doctor seemed to be nodding his approval, so she continued. "If you could see them for nothing, God would repay you a hundredfold." She glanced at his face for his reaction, continuing to describe how much some of these women needed a doctor's care.

Soon he began to smile. "Mrs. Bronstein, you are so convincing I'll have to do it."

Once she began bringing the women to the hospital, one doctor did not seem adequate. Soon her doctor introduced her to others who would help, and slowly this medical ministry expanded. To these women, Esther became their "angel."

More and more, in both the forums and the mothers' group, those who attended spoke out for the new faith they had found—Mrs. Applebaum, the woman who spat on Esther, and many others.

The mission's greatest impetus was its own

converts—many of them the indirect fruit of still another approach: the Bronsteins' kosher table. It wasn't a deliberate strategy. It just seemed to be the thing to do. After a person would come five or six times, he or she or the couple would be invited to the Bronsteins' new flat on Humboldt Boulevard for supper.

Esther's sorrel soup and warm Yiddish conversation broke down barriers; talk and laughter and shared memories brought them together as fellow Jews. Then as Esther cleared the table and the children were dismissed to study or play, gently, subtly, David would dangle the gospel. Maybe he would scarcely talk about it for three or more evenings, until their guests asked to know more. And in the hearing, many gradually became believers.

Not all their associations were pleasant, as Esther reminded David one evening at supper.

"How do you stand that lump, Blind Levin? Week after week he comes to the forum just to make trouble. He talks about atheism and socialism, and he berates anyone who disagrees with him."

"*Nu, nu,* sweetheart! See how he brings the crowd out! A dozen or more come every week just to hear Mr. Levin. We should have more like him!"

Sometimes David's patience could be maddening.

"And Louis Aronson. He's polite, but he is an out-and-out infidel. Is it good to let him speak so much?"

Morris, his fork loaded with hamburger, added the news of the evening. "Reuben's dad, he heard Mr. Aronson speak at the park on Division Street last night. . . . You know what he said? He said he was 'half a Christian'!"

David and Esther exchanged startled glances.

"Half a Christian?" David repeated. "He can do us more harm that way than as a whole infidel. Esther, we'll have him over for dinner next week."

Esther had heard the others talk about Louis Aronson.

As she prepared dinner for his first visit, she thought over what she knew.

He had come from New York City, where he had mingled with many atheists and agnostics. After listening to their orations and reading the literature of Thomas Paine and Robert Ingersoll, he became a full-fledged atheist. When Aronson came to Chicago, he decided to make his living by propagating atheism from soapbox and debate platforms. Soon he had earned the reputation of the leading atheist in the city.

David approached Louis that evening as he did other Jews—through the prophecies of the Messiah and how Christ fulfilled them. For he realized that although Louis thought he was an atheist, the faith of his fathers still lived within him.

He began with Jeremiah 23:3, "Behold, the days come ... that I will raise unto David a righteous Branch, and a King shall reign." Jesus of Nazareth was a descendant of the royal family of David.

He was born in Bethlehem as Micah predicted, and he was born of a virgin, according to the prophecy of Isaiah.

In weeks to come, David went through the Scriptures that portrayed Christ's rejection and crucifixion, Isaiah 53 and Psalm 22.

Finally he discussed the prophecy of Christ's resurrection, Psalm 16:10-11. "For thou wilt not leave my soul in hell; neither wilt thou suffer thine Holy One to see corruption."

He and Louis argued back and forth as David said that Jesus of Nazareth was the Messiah these prophets described. But David never stopped with the prophetic Scriptures. One evening he asked Louis.

"What does the word *Jew* mean?"

Louis had abandoned the religion of his forefathers long ago, so David had to lead him to the answer through various questions and answers. Yes, the name Jew was derived from *Judah* and did not appear in biblical history before the descendents of the tribe of Judah became the ruling family of Palestine. When the Judeans were scattered in other countries, the natives first called them "Judeans," then "Jew" for short.

But there was no stigma to the name Judean or Jew. It came from the word *Judah*, which means "God be praised." How many Christians realized that every time they said "*Jew*," they were saying "God be praised"? Few, if any, they both agreed.

"Seeing as all Jews seem so anxious to remain Jewish, let's talk about what makes a man a Jew," David began another evening.

After pausing to consider what David was getting at, Louis shrugged and replied with the only answer he knew. "A Jew is someone who is born to Jewish parents and follows his father's religion."

As Louis knew, this included him. For modern Jews considered anyone who was born of Jewish parents and did not accept Christianity to be a Jew, whether he was a professed atheist, a communist, or an anarchist.

"And Abraham as the father of the Jewish people was the first Jew. Right?" David continued.

Louis agreed.

"But in Genesis 11:31 we read that Terah, Abraham's father, came from Ur of the Chaldees. He was a Chaldean and not a Jew."

David leaned forward, becoming engrossed in his argument. "And if being a Jew means that someone follows his father's religion, Abraham wasn't a Jew. For in Joshua 24:2, it says that Abraham's father served other gods.... What made Abraham a Jew, then?" David paused to emphasize what he would say next.

"Abraham became a Jew when he heard God's voice

saying to him, 'Get thee out of thy country and from thy kindred, and from thy father's house, unto a land that I will show thee,' Genesis 12:1." David pointed to the verse in his Bible.

"Anyone can become a Jew and a true son of Abraham when he is willing to do what God tells him. That's what God is saying to you, Louis."

David looked at this abrasive, bright young man whom he had come to love. Somehow he knew the Lord would use Louis, if only someone could reach him—and David knew that he was that someone.

"Now listen to me. You listen to me," Louis began, a tone of despair and confusion in his voice. "You want me to commit suicide? To become a *goy*? My education should go to nothing!"

But to David, the desperation in Louis's voice was a sign that the Lord was dealing with him. David had known that pain himself, that fear that he would give in, that Jesus of Nazareth was the Messiah and he could not avoid that truth.

"Right now, Louis, in your pocket you haven't got two cents that you've made with that fancy education, so it's not worth that much to you. But if you accept the Lord, you're going to be different, and you'll really have something. . . . Won't you pray with me?"

Louis had been reading William James's *Varieties of Religious Experiences,* and he had been particularly impressed with James's view that the heart has as much voice as reason. Now his heart, even more than David's words, told him that the time had come, that what David said was true.

And together—still sitting at the Bronsteins' dinner table—David and Louis confessed their love for the Lord Jesus Christ. Not with the same words, but with the same devotion David had felt years before in the home of a

Christian teacher who was now his sister-in-law.

Louis would also relive this moment many times when he led others to the Lord. For soon afterward he enrolled in David's alma mater, McCormick Theological Seminary, and became an ordained minister of the Presbyterian church.

Not all David's and Esther's efforts were this successful. But as often as not, when one member of a family came to know Christ, others followed. . . . All of which makes it sound far too easy. For there were those, too, who became outcasts when they became Christians—shunned by their families, disgraced by the *shul.* Particularly young people. Often, having found faith in Christ, they discovered they had little else.

Many times Esther held a weeping girl in her arms, comforting her as best she could. And their home was often a temporary refuge while a young person got his bearings, found a job, and set his life in a direction that no longer included his family.

The result? Strong Christians. Christians who found their reason for living in study of the Word and in close association with Peniel.

Yes. The name David had given the summer camp in 1921 had become the name of Immanuel Hall in October of 1923.

"It must be Peniel," David said. "The witness and character of our work demand that name."

For in Genesis 32:30, Jacob had named the place of his conversion Peniel, which means "the face of God," because he had "seen God face to face," and his life had been preserved.

"That's what is happening here, Esther. Our people are seeing God's face."

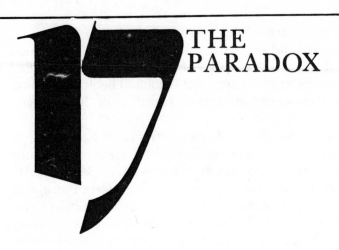

17
THE PARADOX

"THE TURBULENT TWENTIES—those years of Harding and Coolidge when the world teetered unknowingly on the brink of financial disaster—had an electric excitement as jobs and goods multiplied and wages increased. On Chicago's North Side, the occasional automobile became a procession of belching, honking motor cars, and playing in the streets was more hazardous than ever. In the home, household machines like the vacuum cleaner and the washing machine lifted some of the drudgery of Esther's work.

Rural workers moved to the cities to cash in on the plentiful jobs. Immigration slowed; in a few years children of immigrants would outnumber immigrants.

But in the twenties the poorer sections of Chicago—and the North Side was one of them—were still populated by first-generation ethnic groups, people now not so freshly new to the promised land but still struggling with old-country traditions and loyalties.

The Jewish population of the Bronsteins' neighborhood, though increasingly mobile as some continued to up their earnings and move to better areas, was nonetheless constant in numbers. Every few blocks, a synagogue. Between, countless kosher butchers, pushcart peddlers, marriage brokers, and keepers of bookstores, groceries, dry-goods and hardware stores. Here entire Jewish families worked together, the "personnel" of a business they hoped would pay to educate their children and help them move to a better neighborhood.

Yiddish was the language of the streets and stores, and of Peniel—at least among the older participants. Peniel fit into the Jewish community. It did not distance its neighbors with an unfamiliar facade. And people responded.

What did this mean to Esther and David? The demands of their work swirled around them, absorbing, confining, insisting. Yet they maintained the strong sense of family that had been their heritage, but in a different, expanded way. In fact, an observer might have seen Peniel as their family. Certainly the mission was their purpose. Their relationships. Their thought. Peniel regulated and engulfed their family life, yet at the same time was contained by it.

Their preoccupation resulted in a paradox hard to explain, then or now. For they perpetuated their family life in their broader as well as their intimate relationships. Esther, in particular, was the Jewish mother—fanatically loyal not only to her own children but to her brothers and sisters and, beyond that, to her Peniel family. She was the overseeing, maneuvering, possessive, passionately loving matriarch of all she surveyed.

But loyalties and loves so far-spread brought inevitable conflicts in her allocation of time and attention. Her children grew up expecting that mother would spend most evenings away from home; that she would sleep late in the morning while father prepared his only menu, oatmeal; that meals would be irregular, and their home would often be overrun with visitors whom their parents engrossed in long conversations.

David fit the pattern he had brought from the *shtetl:* it was his role to think, to study, to write. And a true scholar he was. His penetrating comprehension of Scripture, particularly as it related to the fulfillment of Old Testament prophecy in Christ, gave substance to their work and depth to their ministry.

But he expected his wife to take care of the practical, everyday decisions—a pattern that not only affected their personal lives but reached into their ministry. She was the driver, the doer—always in motion, forever beginning new programs.

They thrived on this relationship. Esther was content to manage; he was content to be managed. Most of the time. Yet he maintained his position as spiritual head of the home and of their extended home. Where judgments regarding spiritual matters were involved, Esther deferred; where a decision needed the particular leadership of God, Esther assumed her husband's closer connections. Conflicts arose where the practical crossed the spiritual, and sometimes it was a question as to whether Esther's audacity or David's tenacity would win. And where in most Jewish families this arrangement governed only the home, in the Bronsteins' far-extended interests it reached into all their work. David and Esther were the Yiddish father and mother of Peniel and its broadly expanding ministry.

And soon, how that ministry would be financed became an urgent question. Certainly not by the working budget that had always been insufficient. Their needs became even more desperate as they outgrew the small building and needed additional space.

It was Esther who first tapped a deep well of supply.

Mr. Frank Taylor, a vice-president of Continental Illinois Bank, was her target. But as usual, her approach was oblique. People would not give to a cause they did not know, so her first objective was to get him—this busy, important man—to visit Peniel.

It was a spring day in 1923. The older children were in school. David had agreed to watch David, Jr. Esther dressed in her best and caught the streetcar to the elevated train that took her downtown. Impressed but not overwhelmed by the imposing bank building and the plush interior, she asked boldly for Mr. Taylor.

"Have you an appointment?"

"No, but he will want to see me." Well, as a good Presbyterian he would at least know who she was, and they had met once at a church meeting.

Still another receptionist. Then a secretary. And another. The humor of the situation began to get to Esther. When at last the heavy oak doors swung open, she found herself ankle deep in carpet, looking across the polished desk of the great one himself and knowing she couldn't keep the dignity the occasion called for. As they shook hands, she felt laughter rise in her eyes.

"Mr. Taylor." The laughter choked her. "You are harder to see than the president of the United States. This is the sixth place I've been; they just keep walking me."

He laughed with her. Then, obviously busy; he directed the interview toward its purpose. "You came for money, I suppose." He reached for his checkbook.

"No, I came to invite you and Mrs. Taylor to our Friday night forum. We're having Dr. Richardson from the seminary speak, and I think you'd enjoy him." She smiled. "The fact is, Mr. Taylor, we aren't asking for your money. We need you."

Then she heard the monotonous tap of his pencil on the desk edge.

"And what will you do with me?"

"That depends on you." She waited through a long silence, praying, watching the struggle he tried to hide.

Frank Taylor had been impressed by what he had heard of Peniel. Many of his religious and charitable investments brought no such returns. But, another involvement? Another demand on his time?

"I hate meetings. Boards, and things like that."

Esther nodded. "I understand. If you'll just come to the forum sometimes, you can send other people to the meetings."

Her good sense won him over. And that morning began not only the lifetime support of the Taylors but a chain of resulting commitments. For it was Mrs. Taylor who suggested the next step.

"You know, I'd like to bring you a millionaire. If you can get to her, she'll give you money. . . . We wouldn't have to worry so anymore."

"What's her name?" Esther asked, expecting to hear a name like Field or Stone.

"Mrs. David Peck."

Esther was unimpressed and in a hurry to prepare for that night's forum. "I don't know her from Adam," she quipped.

"The Pecks of Bowman Dairy," Mrs. Taylor explained. "They're members of our church. Next time I see her, I'll tell her about you."

146

But later Mrs. Taylor reported that Mrs. Peck was hesitant about the mission. She didn't believe that a Jew could be a Christian.

One summer day Hannah announced the grand lady's arrival.

"Mama! There's a lady outside in a big car with a chauffeur, and she's coming in to see you!"

Esther looked up from the low table where she was helping some young girls with their first sewing lessons. *It's Mrs. Peck,* she thought as she went to the door and looked out. *"Oh, no! This is the end!"*

The limousine had attracted every child from the playground. They walked around, tentatively at first, and then boldly touching the shiny black metal. Soon several palm prints clouded the polished hood.

Esther watched the chauffeur move to reprimand the children. But Mrs. Peck, so lovely, so soft in her summery dress, said, "It's all right, Collins. Just wash the car when we get home." And then she stood and watched as the children took their cue from her and examined the car from bumper to bumper, standing on the running board and peering into the upholstered cab.

I like this woman, Esther decided, and before the visit had ended, Esther felt her warm response. For when Mrs. Peck saw the work—that somebody was finally reaching the people she had always had a fervent, if helpless interest in—she was a friend for life.

Mrs. David Peck became the first president of the Peniel Auxiliary, which organized the women of different Presbyterian churches into a giving and serving group. And the Peck family, along with the Taylors, gave money for many years on a matching-gift basis; they duplicated, dollar for dollar, what others gave. Never again during this period of growth did Peniel suffer from lack of funds.

ESTHER

In 1924 a $25,000 building was erected on the southwest corner of the large lot beside the church; in 1930 another unit would join these two so that they stood as one complete unit facing Washtenaw Street. The remaining portion of the lot continued as a playground. Peniel was destined to become the social and cultural center of the community.

And Esther—her spirit and capability growing as the work grew—was the energetic hub of this giant wheel. Or maybe she was the engine that turned it. Relentless, persevering, untiring—exhausting David and anyone who tried to pace her—she drove an artless, direct route to win her people to Christ.

Not just those at Peniel, but also the Peltz family. If she had her way, every member would be in Chicago and working for Peniel. Already Ruby and Jacob were drawn into the net, and Ida was indispensable.

But she still pursued the other members of the family who had not made a decision for Christ. She visited them, she talked to them, she gave them no rest. Sometimes David marveled at their tolerance. Yet she was like a mother to them, and like most mothers' children they hovered between loyalty and rebellion. You could count on it: when they needed someone, it was Esther they turned to. And she loved it.

Harry, who had been the closest to Esther and David, was a constant and willing target. Even after he had moved to Florida, they managed to get together from time to time. He loved and respected them; he listened, and in the new assurance of his belief he suggested that Esther call a family reunion. Where else but at the Michigan camp?

"Can we do it, David? I don't know how to plan a reunion."

"I've no doubt that you'll manage it, Esther."

Letters went out, and all except Ruth planned to come. They had only seen Morris a few times since they had left Baltimore, but even he had consented. There was one potential bomb: Morris and Ruby. For though Sprintzie had refused their invitation, Jacob would bring Ruby. And to Morris, Ruby was still to blame for the religious division within the Peltz clan. If it hadn't been for Ruby Gaither, they would still be a good Jewish family, living in peace and respect.

Harry was jumpy about Morris for other reasons as well.

"We'd better have devotions in Yiddish, David," he suggested, "and be careful with Morris. We wouldn't want to start any trouble."

The oldest, the richest, and certainly the most overpowering of the family, Morris could ruin an occasion that had been planned with such hopes.

So expectation mingled with dread when the car pulled up, bringing Morris from the train station.

"Morris is here!" Harry called, and Esther hurried down the stairs to be greeted by hugs and kisses from a long-separated brother. Feeling his arms around her made Esther for just a moment not a mother but a little girl. She was in their home in Nikolayev, and her handsome, big brothers had just returned from *shul*. But the moment was fleeting. She was in charge again.

Then Ruby appeared on the stairs.

She saw Morris glance up, his face growing hard and angry. Yet he did not speak. She had been afraid he might shout and demand that Ruby leave. Obviously, he was trying very hard not to ruin the weekend.

Ruby paled, but she walked in the room and sat down with quiet poise. Morris did not say another word. He only paced back and forth, in front of the fireplace. Then he left the room, closing the screen door with elaborate quiet, and began pacing up and down the broad porch outside.

By dinner time, he had calmed somewhat. David gave thanks in Yiddish; the others responded, "Amen." Then Morris added an "Amen," which Esther knew was as close as Morris could come to blessing the event. It was going to be all right.

And it was. Morris loved the lake, the good food, and the deference of his brothers and sisters. Even the devotions seemed to be tolerable to him, and he did not argue with David's Bible lessons. He sat across the table from Ruby without making a disparaging remark. And nobody ruined his enjoyment by pressing him about Christianity.

Only when they were parting at the depot in Holland, Michigan, did Esther express her concern.

"We'll pray for you, Morris, that God will open your eyes."

He answered with a light quip, keeping up a determined show of disinterest.

But he wasn't angry, Esther thought, when, after the last of the family had left, she and David were preparing for the first group of campers.

"It was worth it, David! Someday Morris will listen."

A HOLY NATION

GRADUALLY THE NEIGHBORHOOD around Peniel changed. The familiar sound of women haggling with pushcart peddlers in Yiddish was replaced by a new language—Polish.

The Jewish businesses around Washtenaw had prospered; their proprietors' American dream had come true. They moved to a new neighborhood, Albany Park on Chicago's northwest side. Soon this growing community had a Jewish population of forty thousand, and numerous apartment buildings had sprung up—plus the Kedzie-Lawrence shopping area, with many shops and restaurants—to accommodate the new residents.

David Bronstein was aware of this change, and both he and Esther were confused by it. What did the Lord want them to do?

One day David felt he had received an answer. "Our people are moving to Albany Park, so we will, too."

He had walked that area many times in the last weeks and knew there was no Christian witness nearby.

So David began searching for a building as Esther looked for the money to finance it. But money was short in the spring of 1933, and after weeks of contacting every source she could think of, Esther admitted failure.

"I don't know what to do, David. Is God trying to tell us something? People don't seem to be listening."

Still they kept praying, and Esther continued to talk to anyone who would listen. Then one morning a few weeks later, they received a card from Mrs. Peck.

Dear Mr. Bronstein,
My brother passed away and left a legacy. You may have it for your new building.

David smiled as he read it. "Now you see why no one would listen, Esther. God had another way!"

Esther joined David and some others searching the Albany Park area for an available building. Finally a For Sale sign went up outside a two-story brick structure on Troy Street, about two blocks from the Kedzie-Lawrence intersection.

After talking to a few people, David learned that the building's owner was a Protestant layman who was interested in evangelism. He was selling the building because he was having difficulty getting the tenants to pay their rent. Equipped with this information, David went to see him.

"Are you a Christian?" he asked the gray-haired owner

after he had introduced himself and stated his business.

"Of course, I'm a Christian. A Lutheran, to be exact."

"Well, if you're a Christian, you'll be interested in my proposition," David continued. "I want you to sell me this building. You don't want it if you can't collect the rent. It brings you nothing but trouble."

The owner looked up skeptically from the papers on his desk. "Sell you the building? Have you got the money?"

"Yes, I have. But you have to sell it to me for the mortgage balance. . . . How much is that?" David asked, wondering if he would have that much.

"Five thousand dollars," the owner replied.

"Then I'll pay you $5,000 for it," David vowed, although he had no idea how much Mrs. Peck would send.

"For $5,000, I should sell you the building!" The businessman laughed at David's presumption.

"Not me," David replied calmly. "But the Lord. He will use it to reach the people in this neighborhood who have never heard of Jesus."

"No," the owner wasn't interested. But David persisted. Every week for three months, he returned. At first they only spoke about the property, but soon the man became interested in David's work at Peniel.

When the check from Mrs. Peck came in the mail, it was for $5,000. After thanking the Lord for the accuracy of his beneficence, David began carrying the check in his wallet so he would have it at the appropriate time.

Then one day, the owner admitted, "There must be something behind you, David. For weeks now you've had the nerve to come and tell me I should sell you that building."

"If you don't give me that building, you soon won't collect enough rent to pay the mortgage," David replied, stating what he considered to be a fact rather than a threat. Quickly he drew the check from his wallet and laid it on the man's desk. "This is how the Lord does business."

Within a week, the papers had been signed.

But in its present condition, the building was not appropriate to their needs; a large lecture room was needed, among other things.

So Esther and David had a Swedish carpenter from Maywood go through the building with them as they pointed out the necessary changes. "Seventeen hundred dollars," he estimated.

Seventeen hundred dollars they didn't have. But still they told him to begin, giving him a little money to purchase the supplies. Then they prayed, and Esther began telling people about what the new building would accomplish. Again it was Mrs. Peck who provided the entire amount, even though Esther had been shy of asking her.

David named the new center Aedus, the English transliteration of the Hebrew word for *witness*–following their commission to be "witnesses unto me both in Jerusalem . . . and unto the uttermost part of the earth."

When the building was ready, Esther and David had handbills printed announcing a meeting for men and women that Monday night, and these were passed out to the neighborhood children on their way home from school.

Again they worried about the community's response. Would anyone attend? And if they did, would there be trouble?

Morris, now fully grown, volunteered to stand by the door. "If roughnecks want to come in, I'll stop them," he assured his father.

But the intruders were policemen, not roughnecks.

"Is the man talking up there your father?" they asked

Morris after he had opened the door and identified himself. "If he is, you'd better tell him he's got to quit."

Seeing Morris's immovable expression, the policeman continued. "If he doesn't, we'll move in with the patrol wagon and take you all to the police station."

"Don't worry. I'll tell him," Morris assured the man, scared by his threat. "But let him finish."

"I don't want him to finish," the man who identified himself as the captain demanded.

After protesting that "this is a free country" and receiving only another threat in response, Morris gave in. "OK, I'll talk to my father."

But David would not stop. "Tell him to leave," he told Morris. "I've a message from God, and I'm going to finish it." There was no rancor in his voice, but the look on his face was as determined as the captain's.

Caught in the middle, Morris reasoned with the captain, finally reminding him that he did not have a search warrant. The police left, but not until they had threatened, "You haven't heard the last of this."

The next day David was called to the local police station, where the same captain, who David easily recognized as a Jew, confronted him.

"Look here, Reverend Bronstein, this is a Jewish neighborhood. What are you trying to do?"

"I'm trying to tell the Jewish people the truth about their Messiah," David replied, undisturbed by dissension after years of preaching a belief his people considered heresy.

Without giving the captain an opportunity to respond, he continued. "You mention Jesus, and our people think you mention trouble. I'm trying to tell them the truth—that Jesus is our Savior and one day he will rule the world."

"That I've never heard before," the captain confessed.

"But I tell you, don't do it. People will break your windows, or worse!"

"If they break them, I'll put in new ones," David replied defiantly. "We're not going to cause trouble; we're going to win people because we love them.... I'll give you a book—"

"I don't want your book," the captain shouted as his fist pounded the desk. "Now get out of here, and leave us alone."

"I'll not do that. But I will go see Mr. Lasch if you continue to threaten me."

The captain's face paled at the mention of one of David's parishioners who was a local official and well-known lawyer in Chicago and Washington. But he would not change his attitude, so David left his office to see Lasch.

After David had explained his problem, Lasch called in the captain.

"You know you had no right to say those things or to threaten to stop his meeting." Then he turned to David. "What do you want me to do with him? Remove him from his job?"

"No," David replied. "Just tell him to let me alone."

Mr. Lasch turned to the policeman. "I want you to take care of this man's place. If anyone tries to make trouble, you stop it."

From then on, David had the policeman's protection. But before long the local rabbis began to realize that the center was becoming well established, and the assault became a spiritual one. Quickly they banded together to eradicate this Christian influence. Special articles in the Jewish press attacked Aedus. Mass meetings were held in the synagogues. And again some Jews reacted with a hatred that David and Esther understood even as it wore into their spirit and angered them.

Even the local Communist organization sent a group of ruffians to one of the open forum meetings to terrorize the missionaries. But the young Communists became curious as the meeting progressed, forgetting to voice their objections in their amazement at the sincerity of these Hebrew Christians.

Nothing affected the attendance at Aedus. Not threats. Not curt words to the Bronsteins or their children. Not even a few fights outside the community center. Stubbornly, David continued to hold his forum meetings and extend the center's activities to include study groups and programs for the local children. Soon the majority of the rabbis realized the futility of their opposition, and all but one adopted a policy of passive resistance.

David's methods confounded not only the Jewish rabbis but also the leaders within his own church. For what had begun as a "ma and pa" mission at Peniel was becoming a movement that countermanded authority and ignored precedent. Its increasing strength could no longer be ignored. But was it success? some challenged. David's and Esther's converts were still Jews. Peniel Christians did not conform to the Gentile image of the converted Christian.

And while the Chicago Presbytery wondered about this new expression of Christianity, David began to worry because the majority of his Hebrew Christians who joined Gentile churches were unable to adapt or were not accepted. Many stopped going to church at all. And others drifted away from their faith in Christ altogether.

A survey of Peniel's converts was made, and the results showed that only a small percentage were active Christians. David felt responsible for these converts. He had led them to the Lord Jesus Christ, a belief that launched a spiritual journey. He knew a person could not make this

journey alone—at least not a new convert. Encourage-
ment, fellowship, the love of other believers—Christ's
love within his body here on earth—was needed for
someone to continue the Christian walk. As the missionary who had led them to Christ, David could not abandon
them.

So David and Esther decided to begin taking a group
of their young believers to a church in Humboldt Park.

When the group of twenty young people entered the
foyer of the Presbyterian church, Esther noticed people
looking over their shoulders and talking among themselves. The same rustling and whispering occurred as the
usher showed them to pews at the back of the church.

Soon five or six families throughout the large
sanctuary got up and left. Esther knew why. And although no one suggested that they leave, not one of the
people who clustered around in the foyer afterward
smiled or spoke to them.

Still David and Esther persisted. Every Sunday they
met the others and went to the church; in the evenings
their young people attended the youth group . . . until
one evening when the Jewish teenagers were the only
ones present.

"Why should I go to a church where the pastor hasn't
been able to make his people see that we're all one?"
David said to his friend Dr. Brown at the church extension department.

"It's time you organized a church for your people," Dr.
Brown replied. "Swedes have a Swedish church. Why
shouldn't the Jewish people have a Jewish church?"

And Esther agreed. "You could preach, and the
people could stay afterward for fellowship."

On New Year's Eve of 1934, they invited forty-five
people to their new home in Oak Park for a watch night
service. After prayers and Scripture meditation, David

addressed the group that had assembled.

"We have called you here this evening to start a Christian church for our people, the First Hebrew Christian Church of Chicago."

Before he could go any further, the forty-five Jewish Christians, cramped into the Bronsteins' living room, began to clap. One of the young people who had attended the Presbyterian church with David and Esther spoke the words many others were feeling, "Our own church . . . where we won't be hated because we're Jews."

"We aren't hated by all Christians," David began. "Don't think that. The people in Humboldt Park—and many others—just don't understand Jewish people. That's why they're not in favor of us."

After he could see that the others accepted what he had said, David continued. "Let's try to meet for six months as a Presbyterian church with our own elders and deacons."

The church they founded did not pattern itself after the synagogue or use the Jewish liturgy. The simple Presbyterian service was easily adapted to their needs and spoken in English rather than Yiddish. Occasionally, David would use Hebrew phrases or sentences to lend color or prove a point or show the Christian fulfillment of a Jewish prophecy. But basically the church was not very different from the hundreds of other Protestant churches in Chicago.

After the six month trial period was over, the congregation voted to apply for a charter from the Chicago Presbytery.

"You'll set the church back two thousand years by doing this," some Presbytery officials said, taking their cue from Paul's work among the Gentiles. But David regarded their arguments as further proof of his own: God had revealed that the New Testament Gentile need not first become a Jew to be a Christian. Similarly, in the Gentile church, a Jew need not become a Gentile to be a Christian. Jews and Gentiles, all were one in Christ.

"You are making Judaism Gentile," David accused. "Jesus never did that."

He was well aware that he fought an uphill battle; what he did not know was that forty or fifty years later the Gentile church would catch up with him.

But, despite this dissension, the charter was granted, and the congregation soon grew to sixty-five. For the first time, Jewish evangelism was financed and directed not by Gentiles but by the First Hebrew Christian Church, a group of Jews who believed in Christ but did not break away from the Jewish people. Gone was the old Jewish argument that the Jews who preached Christ to them had been hired by Gentiles to break up Jewish solidarity. Now their own people helped sponsor and direct the work of Peniel and Aedus. And the completed Jew had a Hebrew-Christian home: the First Hebrew Christian Church of Chicago.

One Sunday in September of 1940, a seven-year-old boy complained to David that there wasn't any Sunday school for him like the other Protestants had.

"You bring a friend next week, and I'll provide a teacher," David challenged.

By the end of the year, this method of "bringing a friend" had swelled the class to thirteen, and not long after that to forty.

Slowly the methods and attitudes hammered out in the seclusion of David's study or in the busy streets of Esther's mind worked—which seems far too insensitive a way to describe the transformed hearts and lives that emerged under their joint ministry.

There were mistakes to be sure. There were abortive attempts and relationships gone sour. But through it all ran a cord of passionate love for God and the people he had chosen in Abraham.

David and Esther were not the only persons to see Jewish evangelism as a distinct and different ministry, but they were among the first, and they stand out as the boldest in proclaiming that becoming a Christian in no way repudiated their Jewishness. David preached the Old Covenant as the doorway to the New: he proclaimed, "The Messiah has come!" Then, pointing to their own Scriptures, he proved the claims of Christ to even the most profound Jewish intellect—and that without threatening their identity as Jews. As in New Testament days, his people were Christians *and* Jews.

17 THE SHEKINAH GLORY

SLOWLY, HALF-CONFIRMED REPORTS of unbelievable persecution of relatives left behind in Germany and Poland began to reach the Jewish community. Talk was subdued, as though this would make the reports less probable. Pogroms, the community elders knew about. Organized persecution, they remembered. But death marches? People moved in cattle cars to camps where they were starved, gassed, or shot to death?

No. This was a civilized world, and America was a friend of the Jew. Surely if the American government knew these things, they would not let them happen. But soon a few firsthand reports filtered through, and the

162

meetings after church became long, hushed discussions of the incredible. The impossible.

Then came Pearl Harbor. The young men left in small groups, later in larger ones. The neighborhood suffered through the uncertainty of rationing and the dread of death lists published in the *Tribune*. The lucky ones returned, and with their return came yet another change in community life. They brought a strange restlessness. In fact, nothing stood still anymore—not people, not habits, not life-styles. The Bronsteins watched helplessly as the Jewish community shifted more and more to the north. Those who remained a part of Peniel, Aedus, and the Hebrew Christian Church were now almost entirely second- and third-generation Jewish-Americans.

With the end of the war came the terrible confirmation: the stories were true, more ghastly than imagination could grasp. Scarcely a family but suffered the uncertainty—or the growing certainty—of the agony and death of relatives left behind in Europe. Esther and David ministered to the sorrowing and the angry and welcomed newcomers who bore the grotesque numbers of concentration camps tatooed on their forearms.

The years telescoped, and the work went on. Esther's enthusiasm continued unabated, though she found her failing eyesight an inconvenience.

"It's glaucoma," the doctor said and warned that her sight would become increasingly limited. So she tried even harder.

But in David's case, simply trying could not help. It was a dreadful day when he returned from a doctor's appointment to confirm their worries.

"My heart, Esther. The doctor says I must slow down."

Though a cold fear swept through her, it was quickly past. There was work to be done. Visits to be made. New people hungry to hear about the Messiah! Surely God would overcome this slight obstacle in David's health. Always, the impossible had yielded to her persistence.

"Let's retire, mama," David finally said when he reached sixty-five. He suffered recurring chest pains. He tired easily. But Esther was enjoying her work at Aedus. Ida and her husband, Morris Kaminsky, had taken over the work at Peniel, but there was still so much to be done at Aedus.

David was seventy—and still Esther drove relentlessly as he tried to retreat. Even "a day off" was an unnecessary weakness. Her one concession was their annual trip to Florida. Yet even in Miami—discovering still another Jewish community there—they started a Bible class, and more Jews heard about the Messiah, Jesus.

But back in the complex responsibility of the Chicago work, David realized that he was no longer able to hold things together.

"I may not have many years left, mama, and I want to spend my time in writing and study."

"Always you write, David! And there's work to do."

Their grown children noted that their father would talk to himself, deep in contemplation of a Scripture passage or some new idea he wanted to write about. He would turn phrases over in his mind, trying new expressions, then rush into his study to write down the words that were just right. If only Esther would let him be!

Yet with the pressure to achieve, there was fun—a playful, teasing rapport. Each knew the other so well, and they never fell out of love. David often complimented his wife.

"You look beautiful today!"—as indeed she did, for she always tried to dress in the best of taste. Her hair, gray now, was becomingly arranged; her step was brisk, her smile bright.

Then the time came when Esther reminded David,

"Dearie, our fiftieth wedding anniversary is coming soon. How would you like to buy me a watch?"

"Sweetheart, I'd be delighted to buy you a watch for our anniversary!" And they laughed together at the game they were playing.

Several heart attacks had restricted David's driving, so one winter in Florida Esther learned to drive, though she was now past seventy herself. But because of her failing eyesight, she could no longer keep up the pace she aspired to.

"Write your memoirs, mama," David, Jr., said. Anything to keep her busy!

But deep inside Esther knew that her pushing both of them was a refusal to accept the inevitable. Their ministry was nearing an end. Mortality was as unequivocal a part of their faith as the spirit within them. Soon they would join their Master: the ultimate goal of their lives. Only the going would be difficult.

Sometimes they talked about his leaving her, and David would say with his old humor, "I'm not worried about you, dearie. You'll take care of yourself."

One night—it was late July, 1961—as so often before, they had a meeting in their home, several sitting about the table while David spoke about the Scriptures. Esther, ever the learner when David taught, looked up from her Bible, pained by the weak tremor in his voice. Was she seeing him with new eyes, or was it really so? There seemed a glow around him as he spoke. His face shone with an otherworld light—like the *Shekinah* glory, it was!

Lord, are you going to take my husband? she cried silently.

And there was no answer.

Trying to drive back the gloom, she joined with the family in planning a seventy-fifth birthday party for him, the first party he had ever had. There never seemed to be time before.

ESTHER

The day before the party David complained of more severe pain than usual. With a dread she could not express even to her children, Esther saw him admitted to the nearby Swedish Covenant Hospital. Once there, he felt better.

"I'm having a birthday party tomorrow," he told the doctor. "I've never had one before. I've got to go home for it."

So many times before he had entered the hospital. So many times they had been afraid—and always he had rallied. Yet, even as the doctor said, "You rest here overnight, and if you're better tomorrow, you can go home," Esther felt an unwelcome tightening of her chest that told her this time was different.

Later that night, he suffered a severe attack.

Each day Esther came to see him, and then she would visit other patients on the floor, talking to them about the Lord.

Then one day while she was sitting by David's bed, a woman patient from down the hall came to see her.

"Mrs. Bronstein, there's a Jewish woman in my room who's been listening to some of the things you've been telling us. She wants to see you."

Esther followed the woman back to her room where the other patient was confined to bed. Quietly she began to tell the woman, who could barely lift her head, about Jesus and how he was their Messiah.

"You're not afraid to die, are you?" the woman whispered when Esther finished.

"No," Esther replied. "I know that then I will see my Savior face to face. Then all pain and sorrow will be gone. . . . If you'll just let me pray with you, you can have that assurance, too."

"But what would you say?" the woman asked suspiciously.

"I'm going to pray that you will ask the Lord to come into your heart, so if he takes you tonight, you will go to heaven."

"Not now," the woman resisted. "My daughter is coming tonight, and I want to tell her first." Her voice lowered as her strength faltered. "But, tomorrow. Please come tomorrow."

When Esther returned to David's room, she told him about the woman. "I hope she lives until tomorrow," Esther commented before she went home for dinner.

That evening Esther noticed a change in his condition.

"Don't you feel good?" she asked him immediately.

"I feel weak," he admitted.

"What happened? Tell me. You were all right when I left."

At first David held back, but then he confessed. "After you left, I went to see the woman you had been telling me about. I told her that God had prepared a place for us—her and me. And that when we left our bodies, we would be present with the Lord.

"She said that no one had told her that before, or that the Messiah Jesus could belong to her." David paused, his breath seeming to choke deep within him. "She knew how much I had risked to come, and she had been thinking about what you'd said. . . . She believed, Esther." He looked up at her, his eyes bright. "When I returned to my room, I thanked God that he'd let me finish the work you had begun."

What could Esther say? Scold him for answering this call as he had so many others?

But now she sensed a change in him. A resignation. A quietness of spirit.

He asked for the family, and soon they were all there. Esther looked about at her children and, in the center, pillowed in a chair, her husband of more than fifty years.

ESTHER

Such a mixture of peace and pain she felt! Of pride in his courage. Of faith in their God. Of despair at the thought of living without him.

She listened as he gave each of his children a parting message. Then he added, "I know that you all love the Lord, and I'm not afraid to die," he began slowly. "I know the Lord is going to take me either tonight or tomorrow. He told me so. . . . I have eaten my last meal here on earth. I won't eat again until I am with him."

He asked that they sing "Trust and Obey" together, and as usual, Esther, never bothered by details, got the words confused. David stopped and corrected her. This was his last song on earth, and he would have it right.

When we walk with the Lord in the light of his Word,
What a glory he sheds on our way!
While we do his good will, he abides with us still,
And with all who will trust and obey.

"Now, put me to bed," he said.

Esther heard the children fussing over him, making him comfortable, telling him he'd be home for his birthday cake yet. He let them play their loving game. But when he asked David, Jr., to pray, they wept together.

As she left his room, Esther prayed, *Lord, all the time my husband was in the hospital I prayed that you would make him well. But now I give him up. I can't stand to see him suffer anymore. If you want him, take him.*

At home she continued to pray half the night, and when she awoke at six the next morning, she asked the Lord, *Shall I call the hospital now? Could I take the news?*

You're strong was the answer. *If you want to talk to your husband, call him before I take him.*

At seven o'clock that morning, Esther called and asked for David's room.

"Your husband is not good, Mrs. Bronstein," the nurse replied. "You'd better come."

"Where's his doctor?" Esther asked.

"Standing by his bed as he has since two o'clock this morning."

When Esther got to the hospital, David looked at her through an oxygen tent.

"Sweetheart, come here and hold my hand," he mumbled when he saw her.

Esther held one hand and their daughter, Hannah, the other.

"You know I'm going to be with the Lord," David said again. "You don't want to watch me, do you?"

"No," Esther admitted softly. "But I'd like you to stay a bit longer."

"You'll be all right," he assured her, his words coming slowly as he reached for each breath. "You're brilliant," he said, his voice full of the love and awe he had always felt for her.

"I'm only brilliant because you love me," she whispered, holding back the tears she felt.

Suddenly he pushed off the oxygen tent, looked up at his family, and shouted "Hallelujah!" Even those waiting out in the hall heard his last word, and Esther knew that David had met his Lord face to face.

EPILOGUE

Day by day Esther carried on her work with a strength that scarcely diminished. For time had never conquered her temperament, only toughened it and, paradoxically, tendered it as well.

For four years she continued to direct Aedus. What she lacked in dignity and scholarly persuasion, she made up in love and enthusiasm.

In 1972 a friend from Aedus, Golie Robinson, took her to Israel for her fourth visit—her first trip since the Israelis had reclaimed the Wailing Wall. Slowly Golie led the almost blind, white-haired Esther through the crowd to the wall, the priority of her pilgrimage.

ESTHER

In the glare of the lights that flooded the area, Esther ran her hands over the stones as she knelt and prayed in Yiddish.

I love the Lord my God with all my heart and soul and might. . . . For I have found the Savior, and he is mine.

Esther lived to visit Israel one more time before she died on March 28, 1977, and was buried beside David in the Hebrew-Christian cemetery they helped to found, Acacia Park in suburban Chicago.

But her work and David's goes on. Peniel today is a community center in an increasingly non-Jewish neighborhood, but finding a ministry there with expert, dedicated leadership. The Hebrew Christian Church survives—renamed as *Adat Hatikva* today ("Congregation of Hope"). The church has become a messianic congregation. The ark, the scrolls, the prayer shawl, the yarmulke (skullcap), and Hebrew ritual almost transport one to the synagogue.

Aedus continues as "Sar Shalom." The building is more an office and headquarters than a center, for the Jewish population has moved still farther north. But Aedus still wages a one-to-one ministry. The Jew is brought to Christ not in meetings and movements but in personal, loving, persistent persuasion.

For basically the work at Aedus and Peniel still follows the method, the theology—but more particularly, the attitude—that David and Esther pioneered: "To win the Jew, you must love him."